the world cup

MARK STEWART

FRANKLIN WATTS
A Division of Scholastic Inc.
New York • Toronto • London • Auckland • Sydney
Mexico City • New Delhi • Hong Kong
Danbury, Connecticut

Researched and Edited by
MIKE KENNEDY

Cover design by Dave Klaboe   Series design by Molly Heron

Cover photo IDs: (center) Postage stamp of Uruguay's Alcide Ghiggia; (clockwise from upper left) Diego Maradona on the cover of *Sports Illustrated*; Eusebio on media card; Lothar Matthuas; Jimmy Greaves posing on one knee; Landon Donovan and DaMarcus Beasley on the cover of *Soccer America*; Ronaldo postcard; Zinedine Zidane; Lillian Thurman trading card.

Photographs ©2003: AllSport USA/Getty Images: 79 (Shaun Botterill), 73 (Simon Bruty), 65 right, 69, 71, 75 (David Cannon), 81 (Laurence Griffiths), 44, 50 (Hulton Archive), 61 (Steve Powell), 4 (Ben Radford), 54, 57, 63, 65 left, 74; AP/Wide World Photos: 85 (Gael Cornier), 78, 84 (Thomas Kienzle), 80 (Michel Lipchitz), 82 (Dusan Vranzic), 28 bottom, 30, 35, 51; Corbis Images/Bettmann: 31 bottom, 55 top; Hulton|Archive/Getty Images: 8, 9, 10, 12, 14, 16, 20, 33, 36, 39, 41 left, 45, 46, 48, 52, 55 bottom, 56, 58, 59, 62; Team Stewart, Inc.: all cover photos, 6, 7, 17, 22, 24, 25, 27, 28 top, 31 top, 41 right, 42, 89.

Library of Congress Cataloging-in-Publication Data

Stewart, Mark.
    The World Cup / Mark Stewart. ; researched and edited by MikeKennedy.
    p. cm. — (The Watts history of sports)
    Includes bibliographical references and index.
    Summary: Looks at the history of the world championship of soccer, played every four years since 1930 by athletes from countries on every continent except Antarctica.
    Includes bibliographical references (p.   ) and index.
    ISBN 0-531-11957-2
    1. World Cup (Soccer)—History—Juvenile literature. [1. World Cup (Soccer) 2. Soccer.] I. Kennedy, Mike (Mike William), 1965- II. Title. III. Series.
    GV943.49.S84 2003
    796.334'668—dc21   2003005814

CONTENTS

Soccer's ultimate prize, the Jules Rimet Trophy.

SOCCER GOES GLOBAL

The World Cup

From the very beginning, the World Cup has been more than just a soccer tournament. Acted out on the playing fields and in the stands are the hopes and passions of countries large and small. Every time one nation plays another in this simple game, politics and sports intersect, adding depth and meaning to every save and every score. Each team that makes it to the World Cup has already invested four years of sweat and tears in the process, selecting its top players and molding them into a cohesive unit worthy of wearing its national colors. From there, every victory triggers a celebration; every loss is a reason for national mourning.

While some countries take the World Cup (and soccer) more seriously than others, once the games begin people of all ages and from all walks of life seem to get swept up in it. Almost everyone on the planet has played the sport at one time or another, which makes it the ultimate common experience. Indeed, during the few weeks the World Cup is on, everyone comes a little closer as a species . . . even if they feel like tearing each other apart!

Of course, this did not happen overnight—even a sport as fast-paced as soccer takes time to grow. In fact, the timeline leading up to the first World Cup is nearly 60 years long. It begins in 1872, when England and

Scotland played history's first "international" match. More than three decades later, in 1904, the *Federation Internationale de Football Association*, or FIFA, was formed. At FIFA's 1905 congress, the Dutch representative suggested that a championship tournament be held between the best national teams at the end of each soccer season.

Everyone agreed this was a fine idea, and plans were made to stage this event in 1906. Unfortunately, not a single soccer federation bothered to send in an entry application, so the idea was scrapped for lack of interest. Instead, FIFA decided to recognize the Olympic gold medalist as reigning champions, while continuing to build up popularity and momentum for the sport.

In 1914, at the FIFA congress in Oslo, Norway, a Frenchman named Jules Rimet gained control of the organization. Rimet wanted to revisit the idea of an official FIFA tournament, but his plans were delayed by the outbreak of World War I. After attending the 1924 Olympics, when the national team from Uruguay startled fans with its unique and exciting soccer style, Rimet was convinced that a world tournament would transform his sport.

One day, Rimet bumped into an acquaintance he had made at the Olympics. It was Enrique Buero, an Uruguayan diplomat who, like Rimet, believed very strongly that

A rare color photo from the 1920 Olympic soccer tournament, won by Belgium. Prior to the World Cup, the Olympics provided the only chance for international squads to meet in tournament play.

soccer was poised to become the most popular sport in the world. They got to talking and Buero mentioned that Uruguay might be interested in hosting the first FIFA world championship. A small country wedged between Argentina and Brazil, Uruguay was just beginning to enter the modern industrial age and was anxious for world recognition. What better way than to bring the world to its picturesque capital, Montevideo, than to host FIFA's first championship? The two men talked some more, and Buero offered that the Uruguayan government might also be willing to cover the expenses of the visiting teams—especially for a tournament scheduled for 1930, which would coincide with its centennial celebration.

Excited, Rimet went to work on the details of his plan. He presented the concept of a world championship at FIFA's 1927 congress in Zurich, Switzerland, and the idea was formally accepted. The first "World Cup" would be held in 1930 and every four years after that. FIFA invited

bids from countries interested in hosting the event. At the 1929 FIFA congress, Spain, Holland, Hungary, Italy, Sweden, and Uruguay applied. Holland and Sweden withdrew when they learned of Italy's interest—they felt the Italians could do it better. Uruguay's bid, which the congress was inclined to ignore, got a boost from the Argentinian representative. He gave an empassioned speech that convinced Spain, Hungary, and eventually Italy to withdraw. Uruguay would host the World Cup!

As World Cup 30 approached, the decision to go with Uruguay seemed as if it might turn out to be a mistake. The world economy was in decline, and the steamship voyage (three weeks in some cases) would be expensive and time-consuming. Few teams were willing to give up their best players for two months, and many national federations were too broke to finance the trip. With 60 days to go before the first matches were to be played, not a single European country had formally applied to enter the tournament. When Rimet contacted the various soccer officials, they tried to convince him to switch the World Cup to Rome.

Rimet was furious. All of his work was about to go to waste. Argentina, Bolivia, Brazil, Chile, Mexico, Paraguay, Peru, and the United States had already made arrangements to attend the tournament. It was too late to change venues. These teams were just as angry. Anticipation had been building for the event throughout the Americas, and now they would all look stupid if the Europeans decided not to come. The Latin American federations even threatened to pull out of FIFA.

This threat was very real, and it wouldn't have been the first time it had happened. Years earlier, all of the British countries had withdrawn from FIFA in a squabble over the difference between amateurs and professionals. Their absence from the World Cup throughout the 1930s would rob the tournament of some prestige, as many of the world's best players performed in the British Isles.

Facing personal and professional ruin, Jules Rimet went to work twisting arms and calling in favors. He managed to talk Belgium, France, Romania, and Yugoslavia into going to Uruguay, with the promise that the host country would be picking up the tab. Thus, of the 13 teams that arrived in Uruguay for the inaugural World Cup, nine hailed from the Americas.

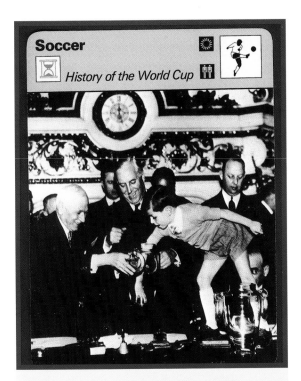

This vintage Sportscaster card captures the 1938 World Cup draw. Jules Rimet (left) watches as his nephew plucks team names out of a glass container.

1930 Uruguay

FIFA arranged the 13 national squads into four pools, each of which would conduct a round-robin schedule before sending a single pool winner into the semifinals. The final was scheduled for Centenario Stadium, even though it was still under construction when the opening-round matches began.

Uruguay was one of two pre-tournament favorites. Besides being the World Cup host, the team had a pair of potent scorers in Luis Monti and Pedro Cea. And goalkeeper Jose Andrade gave the defense a lot of confidence with his play in net. Argentina figured to have a strong team, too. Pancho Varallo supplied veteran leadership as well as a spark on offense. He was joined by a youngster named Guillermo Stabile. Known as *"El Infiltrador"* (the Infiltrator), he could penetrate almost any defense with his slick dribbling and dazzling speed. This dynamic duo had the potential to carry the Argentinians all the way.

Beyond these two South American powerhouses it was anyone's guess. International soccer was still very new, and no one had enough information about all the teams to predict with any accuracy how they would do. Yugoslavia seemed to have decent players, and the French put a good team on the field, too. The United States, a "baby" in soccer terms, mostly sent big, brawny athletes to compete. Their soccer skills were a notch below everyone else's, however they were nothing if not enthusiastic.

Size and enthusiasm don't often count for much on a soccer field, but at World Cup 30 they most certainly did. Led by Bert Patenaude, the U.S. scored 3-0 victories over Paraguay and Belgium, thanks to their tenacity and willingness to body slam opponents. The French players watched the Americans with great amusement, and called them the "shot-putters" for their heavy-handed approach.

As expected, Yugoslavia and Uruguay also emerged from their opening-round pools. Argentina got a scare from France, which was prevented from tying the score late in the game by a referee's blunder. Misjudging the clock, he signalled the end of the game just as France was zeroing in on the Argentine goal. There were actually three minutes remaining. When play resumed, Argentina kept France bottled up to preserve a 1-0 win. The semifinal matches featured a couple of blowouts. Uruguay torched Yugoslavia 6-1, as Cea scored three times, while Argentina defeated the U.S. by the same score.

Uruguay, the first World Cup champions. Their country hosted the 1930 tournament hoping to generate worldwide publicity for the little-known South American nation.

South America's overwhelming passion for soccer was evident in the build-up for the first World Cup final. The entire continent was abuzz, and the rivalry between neighboring Uruguay and Argentina (their capital cities are separated by less than 200 miles) grew in intensity as kickoff neared. Everything seemed to start an argument, something as trivial as whose ball was to be used.

The Argentinians despised Monti, whom they felt was a dirty player, and they were not shy about sharing this opinion. When it was revealed four days before the final that the Argentinian star Varallo had a broken foot, it touched off a national celebration in Uruguay. Angered by this response—and loathe to show any signs of weakness—his coach ordered him to play anyway.

By game day, the possibility of rioting was very real. The only thing separating Uruguay and Argentina is the Rio de la Plata (River Plate), making it easy for Argentina's fans to attend the final. Everyone who entered Centenario Stadium (which was finished in the nick of time) was searched for firearms by the police.

The match started badly for Argentina when Varallo tried to make a cut and collapsed in agony. He limped to the bench, where he tended to his injury. Taking advantage of his absence, Uruguay's Pablo Dorado scored to put his team up, 1-0. Argentina refused to quit. Carlos Peucelle evened things up, then Stabile followed with a goal that gave Argentina a 2-1 lead. Uruguay claimed the play should have been disallowed because the Argentinians had been offsides. The referee disagreed and the goal stood. Argentina took a 2-1 lead into the locker room at intermission.

The first half had been played with Argentina's ball. Now Uruguay's was put into play. Although there was no obvious difference between the two, Uruguay seemed immediately at ease and began playing with renewed confidence. Cea knotted the score

Argentine goalie Botasso lunges for a ball in the 1930 final. He let in four goals, while his Uruguayan counterpart, Jose Andrade, allowed only two.

BEST OF THE BEST

Who plays on a World Cup team? That is up to each country's soccer federation. Because a World Cup team is a "national" team, it should feature the nation's best players. They are chosen in the months leading up to the tournament by the national coach, who is also appointed by a country's soccer federation. This process can be very controversial, because a coach might favor certain players over others, and the fans might not agree.

In the early days of the World Cup, each nation put together a team of "all-stars" from its various amateur and pro leagues. But with the worldwide spread of the professional game, a country's greatest players might be playing in another country. This had a good side and a bad side.

Obviously, players performing against the best international competition were of great value in the World Cup. But it is not always easy to blend their skills and egos with those of homegrown players. On occasion, national team coaches have passed over big stars in favor of players they could develop as part of a team concept. The results have been mixed. Sometimes this idea has led to a championship, while occasionally it has led to disaster.

Whatever the strategy, the selection of World Cup teams has become one of the most-watched and hotly debated aspects of the build-up for the tournament. And with good reason. Time and again, the "last" player to make a club has gone on to accomplish incredible things.

FIFA president Jules Rimet presents the World Cup trophy to Paul Jude, president of the Uruguayan Football Association, after his team beat Argentina in the final.

at 2-2, and 10 minutes later Santos Iriarte put Uruguay ahead with another goal.

On the Argentine bench, Varallo decided it would be more painful to watch than to play. He re-entered the game, still limping, hoping to inspire his teammates, who were beginning to drag. The gesture worked, and Argentina picked up the pace. Late in the game, Varallo booted a hard shot toward Uruguay's net. Andrade lunged at the last instant, and knocked the ball away. To some, it appeared the ball had crossed the goal line before Andrade punched it out. Argentina argued this point furiously. When their appeal was denied, the team lost its wind and Uruguay added a fourth goal to nail down the 4-2 victory.

The Uruguayans had not only put on a good tournament, they had won it. Rimet and the FIFA staff could not have been more pleased with the outcome. They knew every country in the world would soon be begging to host the World Cup. Despite a few faults and a scary moment or two, the first World Cup proved a smashing success.

> **Winner: Uruguay**
> **Runner-up: Argentina**
> **Best Player: Pedro Cea**

1934
Italy

The success of the first World Cup produced an unexpected response: no fewer than 32 teams wanted to play in 1934. Although worldwide economic conditions were worse than ever, soccer's popularity was soaring. Many countries believed it was worth the cost to support a strong national team, because it gave people something to get excited about. To accommodate all the entries, FIFA staged a series of qualifying matches (as it does to this day) to determine the final 16 teams. These "finalists" would then compete in a single-elimination format (you lose, you go home) with games tied after overtime to be replayed on another day.

Italy was awarded the tournament after the two front-runners—Spain and Hungary—withdrew their bids in 1932. Sweden had also expressed an interest in hosting World Cup 34, but later removed its name from consideration. FIFA was not particularly keen on Italy. Fascist dictator Benito Mussolini was bent on restoring the ancient glory of the Roman Empire, and seized upon any opportunity he could to produce a massive spectacle. Jules Rimet did not want Il Duce (who didn't even like soccer) to turn his tournament into a propaganda event, but beggars can't be choosers and because of all of the withdrawals, Italy had become the only game in town.

The World Cup triggered a massive building campaign in Italy. With the whole world coming, Mussolini wanted his country to be a showplace. Dozens of beautiful new public buildings were constructed, as was a new stadium, the National Fascist Party Arena in Rome. It would later be used for massive political and military rallies. Mussolini also wanted Italy to win the World Cup. He summoned the president of the country's soccer federation to his palace, and made this clear. If the president wanted to remain head of the organization (or perhaps not lose his head) nothing short of victory would be acceptable.

The man charged with molding this team was Vittorio Pozzo, the national coach since 1929. Though he had never played

Vittorio Pozzo gets a ride on the shoulders of his jubilant players. Their victory over Czechoslovakia brought the World Cup to Italy.

competitively, Pozzo possessed amazing instincts for the game, both in devising strategy and spotting talent. In his five years at the helm, the team had become a European powerhouse. A big part of Pozzo's success resulted from Italy's liberal citizenship laws. Anyone who could trace their family heritage back to Italy could apply for dual citizenship. Thanks to the country's long-time business relationships with South American nations, it was easy for, say, an Argentinian soccer star to show he had "Italian blood" somewhere in his family. And that meant he could play on the Italian team.

Two of these "imports" anchored the Italian club in 1934. Luis Monti, who starred for Uruguay in the first World Cup, was now the leader of Italy's defense. For-

ward Raimondo Orsi, from Argentina, transformed the Italian offense with his creative play on the wing. He worked beautifully with native Italians Giovanni Ferrari and Giuseppe Meazza, who was the biggest star on the team. Italy's greatest strength may have been its goalkeeper, Gianpiero Combi, who is still regarded as one of the best players in this position.

Italy expected its main competitor to be the Austrian "Wunderteam." Unbeaten in its previous 18 matches, Austria came into the tournament after having humbled some of the world's top national teams, including Italy on its own home turf. The mastermind of this bunch was coach Hugo Meisl. He and Pozzo were the reigning soccer geniuses in Europe during the

1930s, elevating the game by developing new strategies and coaching techniques. The Austrians may have been a bit past their prime by World Cup 34, but they were still great. Rudi Hiden was a terrific goal-keeper, Johan Horvath was a dangerous scorer, and the impossibly skinny Matthias Sindelar—known as the "Man of Paper"—had an uncanny knack for being in the right place at the right time when his team's precise, short-passing attack was working.

Spain and Czechoslovakia were both strong, too. The Spaniards relied on their legendary goal-keeper, Ricardo Zamora, who could dominate a game from the net.

The Czechs, who played a style similar to Austria's, had opened the eyes of soccer fans months earlier by beating England. The tandem of Oldrich Nejedly and Antonin Puc gave opponents fits. Uruguay, still smarting from Italy's refusal to travel to World Cup 30, returned the favor by declining to defend its championship on Italian soil.

The first round proceeded without any upsets, though Austria needed a goal in extra time to dispose of France. The Italians romped, 7-1, over a weak team from the United States, while Spain and Czechoslovakia also won with relative ease. For every loser it was a short, unhappy stay in

A FIRST TIME FOR EVERYTHING

For obvious reasons, World Cup 30 was the site of many—but not all—World Cup firsts. Here's a look at some of the most memorable ones . . .

First Game: France 4, Mexico 1, Montevideo, Uruguay, July 13, 1930

First Goal: Lucien Laurent, France, July 13, 1930

First Two-Goal Game: Andre Maschinot, France, July 13, 1930

First Ejection: Mario de Las Casas, Peru, July 14, 1930

First Three-Goal Game: Guillermo Stabile, Argentina, July 19, 1930

First Player to Compete for Two Countries: Luis Monti, Argentina, 1930 & Italy, 1934

First Draw: Italy 1, Spain 1, Florence, Italy, May 31, 1934

First Televised Game: Yugoslavia-France, Lausanne, Switzerland, June 16, 1954

First Trading of Jerseys After Game: World Cup 54

First Team to Win the World Cup on Another Continent: Brazil, 1958; Sweden

First Player to Score in Consecutive Championship Games: Vava, Brazil, 1958 & 1962

First World Cup Mascot: World Cup Willie, England, 1966

First Three-Goal Game in a Championship Final: Geoff Hurst, England, July 30, 1966

First Substitute to Score: Juan Basaguren, Mexico, June 7, 1970

First Red Card: Carlos Caszely, Chile, June 14, 1970

GREAT COACH:
VITTORIO POZZO—ITALY

In the early years of World Cup play, the indisputable king of coaches was Vittorio Pozzo, who took over the Italian national team in 1929 and led it to the championship twice during the 1930s. Soccer was not a popular sport in Italy during the early years of the 20th century, so Pozzo never gave it much thought. While studying in England, however, he fell in love with the game as he sat in the stands and rooted for Manchester United and its star midfielder, Charlie Roberts.

When Pozzo returned to Italy he set out to spark a soccer revolution, and eventually was named coach of the Olympic team in 1912. He befriended Austria's Hugo Meisl and England's Herbert Chapman—both visionary coaches—and built on what he learned from them. His national team won the World Cup in 1934, the Olympics in 1936, and the World Cup again in 1938.

Criticized by some for his liberal use of South Americans, Pozzo responded by saying that these same men were also eligible for military service. "If they can die for Italy," he pointed out, "they can play football for Italy."

Vittorio Pozzo shows off his second World Cup trophy. Italy was the dominant nation in European soccer during the 1930s.

Italy. Indeed, teams such as Brazil and Argentina (which traveled thousands of miles to compete) faced a long trip back across the Atlantic after losing their opening-round matches.

The action heated up in the quarterfinals. Austria slipped past Hungary, 2-1, while the Czechs narrowly beat Switzerland, 3-2, and Germany eked out a one-goal victory over Sweden. These matches were close, well-played and extremely exciting. However, none compared to Italy's hair-raising quarterfinal experience with Spain. A macho battle full of intimidation and posturing, the game featured several great saves by Zamora to keep Italy off the scoreboard for the entire first half. Spain took a, 1-0, lead into intermission thanks to a nice shot by Luis Regueiro. The hard fouling continued in the second half, as the increasingly desperate Italians struggled to solve Zamora. Finally, the Spanish keeper made a mistake, giving up a rebound off a shot by Mario Pizziolo after Meazza bumped into him. Ferrari blasted the ball into the net to even the match. When no one scored the rest of the game, a replay was scheduled for the following day.

For their second meeting, Italy put four fresh players in its starting lineup, while Spain substituted seven. Again, both teams played great defensive soccer. Meazza's first-period header past a diving Zamora was the only score in the match, as Italy moved on to the semifinals. There they would play the Austrians in the marquee match of the entire competition. Italy was installed as the favorite for two reasons: first, Horvath was injured and could not play for Austria; second, the field was muddy, which would slow the Austrian attack.

The Italians got a goal in the 18th minute when Meazza again bumped the keeper. The play occurred on a corner kick, which Hiden failed to pluck out of the air. The ball skittered through to Enrico Guaita, who deposited it in the net. The defense held off Sindelar and company the rest of the way to make the lone goal stand up, and Italy was in the final. The other semifinal, between Czechoslovakia and Germany, was not nearly as close. Nejedly was unstoppable, with a pair of goals. Puc played brilliantly, too, and the Czechs won, 3-1.

Italy faced a formidable challenge in stopping this pair. They also had to contend with a red-hot keeper named Frantizek Planicka. Jules Rimet took his seat next to Mussolini for the final and watched as the Italian team gave Il Duce the stiff-armed Fascist salute. The two barely exchanged a word during the match, which was just fine with Rimet. He was extremely pleased with number of press credentials that were issued for the match. Some 270 journalists from around the world were covering the World Cup—many times more than had shown up in Uruguay four years earlier. As distasteful as he found the host country's politicization of soccer, he realized that ultimately this great spectacle would be good for the sport.

The first half of the game was played slowly, cautiously, and nervously by both teams. Neither wished to make a mistake, and settled for probing each other for weaknesses. There were only a handful of good shots in the opening 45 minutes, and no goals were scored. The Czechs were satisfied with this pace, for they knew the longer it took Italy to score, the more pressure its players would feel.

The second half went nearly 30 minutes before the game's first goal was scored. It came off the foot of Puc, who broke through

Vittorio Pozzo (far left) confers with two of his players with the final deadlocked at 1-1 after 90 minutes. The Italians scored twice in extra time.

the Italian defense and knocked the ball past Combi. Moments later, the Czechs nearly scored again, but hit the post. Italy tied the score with less than 10 minutes left, when Orsi mistimed a shot and sent it spinning wildly off to one side. A stunned Planicka took a second to recover, by which point the ball was curling across the goal line. The next day Orsi tried to recreate the crazy, corkscrewing shot for puzzled reporters but gave up after several dozen unsuccessful attempts.

A 30-minute overtime followed, during which Pozzo decided to give Orsi a rest by having him exchange positions with Angelo Schiavio. The move worked better than the Italian coach could have dreamed when Guaita hit Schiavio with a perfect pass which he drove past Planicka. Italy held on for a 2-1 win and the championship.

Winner: Italy
Runner-up: Czechoslovakia
Best Player: Giuseppe Meazza

1938
France

In the four years since World Cup 34, much had changed in the world. Benito Mussolini was no longer top man on the Fascist totem pole. He had been surpassed by Adolf Hitler, whose dreams of Nazi expansion were already starting to change the colors on European maps. With the continent on the precipice of war, soccer was viewed by many leaders as a vehicle for national pride and ambition.

This became crystal clear when Germany

annexed its neighbor, Austria, and Austria politely informed FIFA it would not be participating in World Cup 38, because it was no longer a country. Hitler made the most of this situation, seeing to it that the best Austrian players were incorporated into the German national team. In his mind, this practically guaranteed that Germany would win the World Cup. The desire for a soccer championship had become very important to der Fuhrer after his experience as host of the 1936 Olympics. Staged in part as a tribute to Aryan supremacy, the games instead ended up showcasing the skills of African-American athletes such as Jesse Owens, Ralph Metcalfe, and Mack Robinson, the older brother of Jackie Robinson.

Needless to say, the pressure on the German players to win was intense. For the Ital-

ian players, the stakes were even higher. The consequences of losing were spelled out in no uncertain terms. Prior to the opening matches the team received a three-word telegram from Mussolini himself. It read "WIN OR DIE."

Since its championship in 1934, the Italian team had also earned an Olympic medal. The team blended youth with experience, which was a huge advantage in World Cup play. Coach Vittorio Pozzo still had two key players from the '34 squad in Giovanni Ferrari and Giuseppe Meazza, as well as Uruguayan imports Michele Andreolo and Silvio Piola.

Hungary also had a fine team. Led by Pal Titkos, the squad managed to spice up its methodical approach with a flashy play from time to time, and were a lot of fun to

Politics and soccer are sometimes difficult to separate. The Italian team salutes German dictator Adolf Hitler after winning the 1936 Olympic championship in Berlin.

watch. Another team that drew attention was the Dutch East Indies, Asia's first representative in World Cup play. Japan was planning to take this slot, but pulled out of the qualifying process after its army invaded China.

The class of the South American teams was Brazil. Its star was Leonidas Da Silva. Nicknamed the "Black Diamond," he was the first player to perfect the bicycle kick, which enabled him to launch strong, accurate kicks with his back to the defense. Coach Ademir Pimenta looked to a sparkling forward named Tim for offense, while fullback Domingos da Guia was given the responsibility of marking the top enemy scorer.

Absent from the action were Argentina, Colombia, Costa Rica, Mexico, El Sal-vador, and Surinam. Argentina had campaigned vigorously to host World Cup '38, but FIFA President Jules Rimet selected France instead—a country less interested in soccer than in its two favorite sports, rugby and cycling. Sensing that international soccer had reached a new high in popularity, Rimet chose his home country over soccer-mad Argentina in the hope that he could catapult the sport to national prominence. It mattered little to him that France was preparing for war with Germany, or that bombs were dropping just over the border in Spain. The time was right and he wanted to pounce on the opportunity.

Argentina was so furious at this slight that its soccer federation boycotted the tournament. Then it launched a campaign to keep its neighbors out. Even the United

POWER PLAYER: GIUSEPPE MEAZZA—ITALY

Only two players performed for both of Italy's World Cup winners during the 1930s. Inside forward Giovanni Ferrari was one, and Giuseppe Meazza—the team's other inside forward—was the other. Though both were world-class players in every way, Meazza was the preeminent striker of his generation.

At World Cup 34, it was Meazza's play that made the difference in both first-round games against Spain, and he played a key role in the win over Austria. At World Cup 38, Meazza and Ferrari were hypnotic in the final against Hungary, setting up Piola for the game winner.

Meazza's brilliance was not limited to muscling his way to the net and scoring, although this was a specialty. Instead, what distinguished him from his contemporaries was his willingness to withdraw from the action and create opportunities for others. This he did by passing, heading, decoying, or just plain intimidating opponents. Meazza could read the field and make quick decisions. Although nothing made an enemy defender's eyes widen like the sight of Meazza bearing down on him, nothing made a defender sweat like not seeing him at all.

States sided with Argentina, and declined to send a team. Ultimately only 15 nations participated in World Cup 38.

Because of this odd number, the format of the tournament was tweaked to eliminate seven countries in first-round matches, with the eight survivors making up a field of quarterfinalists. Sweden was given a bye. Once again, FIFA moved to prevent draws by having matches replayed in their entirety if they could not be decided in overtime.

This "replay" system immediately came under scrutiny when unheralded Switzerland battled the imposing Germans to a 1-1 tie. The result was embarrassing enough for Germany, which was still struggling to mesh the talents of its German and Austrian stars. What followed was disastrous: Switzerland actually beat Germany in the rematch, 4-2. Coach Sepp Herberger had plenty of explaining to do when he and his players returned to Berlin.

Italy nearly suffered the same fate in its first game against Norway. The game started on a sour note for the Italians, who were roundly booed by hundreds of fans who had fled Italy for France because of the repressive Fascist regime. Although Italy scored first in this match, Norway controlled the action for most of the game thanks to the relentless attacking of its center-forward, Knut Brunyldsen. Three would-be goals clanked off the post, and a score was waved off by officials who ruled the shooter offsides. Norway finally netted the equalizer, then nearly scored again. Only a spectacular save by Aldo Olivieri preserved the tie. Piola scored in overtime to give Italy a 2-1 win.

Brazil, meanwhile, won a wild one against Poland in the rain. Da Silva confounded the Poles with a hat trick in the first half. But Ernst Wilimowski rallied his

troops with three of his own. Da Silva scored again, kicking the ball with his stocking foot after his shoes came off in the mud, but the Poles hung tough and the game went into overtime. Brazil finally won, 6-5. Hungary and France also moved on, though much more conventionally—the Hungarians beat the Dutch East Indies 6-0, while the French cruised past Belgium, 3-1.

The action wasn't quite as exciting in the quarterfinals. Sweden, playing in its first game of the tournament, blasted Cuba, 8-0. Hungary defeated the upstart squad from Switzerland, 2-0. And Italy began to round into form, beating France 3-1 after Pozzo made some key substitutions. The most hotly contested game was the Brazil-Czechoslovakia match. It was tightly played, with lots of fouls. Three players were ejected and the game ended in a 1-1 tie. The replay went to Brazil, 2-1, after Pimenta replaced nine of his 11 starters.

Da Silva played in both games. He was a small, wiry fellow who did not stand up well to rough tackling. He was so beaten-up and exhausted by the two Czechoslovakia matches that he could not play in the semi-final against Italy. Tim was also too tired to play. Rumors immediately started circulating that the cocky Brazilians were so sure they could beat Italy that they were resting their two best scorers for the final. Coach Pozzo knew this was not true, but used the story to motivate his players.

The game opened with da Guia shadowing Piola, which threw the Italian offense into disarray. But Italy's defense played well and neither team scored in the first half. In the second half, Pozzo decided to use Piola as a decoy. Time and again he lured da Guia out of position and let his teammates exploit the opening. Gino Colaussi finally broke the ice with a goal to put Italy ahead, 1-0.

Emboldened, Piola took a poke at da Guia when the referee's back was turned. When da Guia returned the blow, the referee was right on it and whistled him for the foul. Meazza took the shot and scored—and then his pants fell down! They had been torn earlier in the game and his teammates had to form a wall around him until a new pair was produced. Brazil managed to score a goal when the action resumed, but that was all and the Italians were in the final.

In the other semifinal, Hungary had a much easier time with Sweden. After the Swedes scored a quick goal, the Hungarian offense unloaded on them, scoring three times. In Sweden's desperation to close the gap, its defense allowed two more Hungarian goals, resulting in a 5-1 win.

The final, which drew an impressive crowd to the Stade de Colombes in Paris, featured two dynamic and well-coached clubs. The Italians got on the board first on a goal by Colaussi. Titkos evened the score just a minute later, but Italy was undaunted. Meazza and Ferrari began working a two-man scheme that befuddled the Hungarian defenders and produced a chance for Piola, who scored the go-ahead goal in the 15th minute of play. Colaussi scored again before the half to make it 3-1 Italy.

Hungary came out attacking in the second half, and after 20 minutes they had a goal off the foot of Sarosi. The Italians remained calm and counter-attacked, setting up Piola's second goal of the day. The score remained 4-2 the rest of the way, as Italy won its second World Cup and the Italian players lived to fight another day. After the match Hungarian keeper Szabo shocked reporters by saying it was the proudest day of his life. "We may have lost the match," he explained, "but we have saved 11 lives."

Italy's Alfredo Foni attemps to control the ball in midair, as a Hungarian defender looks on.

1950
Brazil

A lot had happened in the dozen years since the last World Cup had been contested. Millions of people had perished in the Second World War, new nations had been born, several countries had had their borders redrawn, and a handful had been swallowed up in the political struggles that followed.

Brazil was chosen by FIFA to host the tournament on the strength of its bid for World Cup 42—an event that obviously never came off. Despite a lot of lead time, the Brazilians struggled to complete their preparations. The centerpiece of their bid, the 175,000-seat Maracana Stadium in Rio di Janeiro, was barely ready. When fans filed in for the opening-round matches, they were surprised to see exposed girders and other signs that the job had not quite been completed.

The field for World Cup 50 was thinner than anticipated. While the Americas were relatively prosperous in the postwar years, Europe was still struggling to recover from the devastation the war had caused. Among the nations that simply could not afford to send a team were Scotland, Germany (now West Germany), Austria, France, and Portugal. When the Soviet Union turned down FIFA's invitation to compete, the countries that had fallen within its sphere of influence—including East Germany and Hungary (which had a marvelous team)—followed suit. The only Eastern Bloc squad to make

the trip was Yugoslavia, which never took kindly to foreign rule and actually seemed to enjoy thumbing its nose at the Russians. Missing from the South American sphere was Argentina, an undeclared ally of Germany and Italy during the war.

When all was said and done, only 13 squads chose to travel to Brazil and compete in the event. FIFA responded by creating four pools, two with four teams, one with three teams, and the other with only two teams. A quartet of clubs would then advance to the Final Pool, where a round-robin tournament would determine the champion. This odd arrangement meant that a traditional "final" might not take place.

The unorthodox format and weak field made England a big favorite. The English squad featured a powerful lineup that included two of the greatest players in the country's history. At 35, Stanley Matthews could still dribble the ball as well as anyone in the world. Few players, meanwhile, could match the all-around talents of Tom Finney. They were the stars on a solid, all-around team that also included Stan Mortensen, Billy Wright, Roy Bentley, Jimmy Mullen, and Wilf Mannion—the first team that England had ever entered in World Cup competition.

There was definitely hope for the other countries. They reasoned that the strange environment might throw England off its game. Also, the Brits were not the same since losing fullback Neil Franklin. He had left England to play for a professional club in Colombia, and thus was ruled ineligible by his own soccer federation.

Brazil was the class of the South American teams. Drawing from a deep talent pool that was unaffected by the war, coach Flavio Costa had assembled an excellent group of players. Forwards Ademir, Jair, and Zizinho were like conjurers when they were playing well together. With the home fans cheering them on, this trio seemed poised to dominate the entire tournament. The only question was what they could accomplish against England.

There was little else to excite the fans beyond these two teams. Not much was known about the young players who had come up after the war, while the more familiar names and faces on the various rosters were all in their 30s by this time. Italy had hoped to field a crack squad, but a plane crash one year earlier had claimed the lives of eight of their key players. The new guys,

Stan Mortensen, one of the many stars on England's first World Cup team. He was still a hot item with card collectors two generations later.

though talented, had not yet gelled with the survivors. Sweden had a perfectly good team on paper, but their lack of a big star and a boring style turned fans off.

Uruguay always seemed to have a good team, but this one appeared to be an exception to that rule. Initially, the country had failed to qualify, and only received an invitation when Peru and Ecuador dropped out. Unlike the Swedes, however, the Uruguayan team was fun to watch. Captain Obdulio Varela never stopped running, and goal-keeper Roque Maspoli had days when no shot got past him. A young defender named Victor Andrade was being touted as a future star, while forwards Juan Schiaffino and Alcide Ghiggia supplied some offensive punch. Beyond these five, however, there was little to suggest that Uruguay could hold its own against the better teams.

The fans may have been expecting a ho-hum tournament, but from the outset it seemed clear that this would not be the case. In Pool 1 action, Italy authored a 2-1 lead against the listless Swedes only to watch in horror as the Swedes suddenly came to life and beat them. In Pool 2, England dusted off Chile 2-0 and then "prepared" for its match with the United States by taking a day off. The Brits had every reason to be confident. Theirs was the finest team in the world. The Americans were so bad that their top scorer, Joe Gaetjens, had been washing dishes in a Brooklyn restaurant a month earlier. It happened to be the same place where the U.S. team gathered for team meals, so he asked coach Bill Jeffrey for a tryout. Gaetjens quickly became its best player, leading a nothing-to-lose collection of young men whose "real" jobs ran the gamut from carpenter to mail carrier to interior decorator.

Looking to take another afternoon off, England started the game hoping to score quickly. The English players swarmed all over the American defense, getting off a dozen clear shots. They missed an easy goal when a shot hit the post. Then goal-keeper Frank Borghi made a couple of nice saves. The Americans, clearly astonished at their good fortune, began smiling. English coach Alf Ramsey was clearly annoyed; the last thing these Yanks needed was a shot of confidence.

The Americans attacked, at first tentatively but soon they were playing like they meant it. In the 37th minute, Walter Bahr (whose sons Matt and Chris would play college soccer and then star as place kickers in the NFL) launched a shot from 25 yards. Keeper Bert Williams glided over to catch the ball, when it grazed the head of Gaetjens and changed direction just enough to elude Williams and land in the net. It almost looked as if the American forward had been trying to get out of the way of Bahr's shot. But this may have been a practiced play. Either way, the best team in the tournament had failed to take the worst team seriously, and it had cost them a goal.

For the rest of the game, the American defenders stuck to their opponents like glue. With each foiled English scoring attempt, the buzz in the stadium grew louder and the Brits grew more uncomfortable. They were used to being booed on enemy soil, but they had the distinct impression that they were being laughed at now. Unable to score, they went down to a humiliating 1-0 defeat.

When news reached England, most fans thought the score was a misprint. A 10-1 game made more sense than an 0-1 game. Needing a win to stay alive, England dropped its next game to Spain by the same score. When they returned home the English players were greeted with the newspaper headline "British Football Is Dead."

Another powerhouse that stumbled was the home country, Brazil. After shutting out Mexico 4-0, the best the team could do was gain a tie with Switzerland. A loss to Yugoslavia in the next game would mean elimination, so the entire nation took up the cause and launched a campaign called "Save Brazil." Past heroes came forward to lead enormous pep rallies, and the players on the national team were treated like kings. They responded by winning 2-0, but not without an assist from their unfinished stadium. On the way out to the field, one of Yugoslavia's key players, Rajko Mitic, clipped the top of his head on an exposed steel beam. By the time he was stitched and bandaged, his team was already down a goal.

As competition in the Final Pool began, Brazil began to play great soccer. In wins over Sweden and Spain, the team looked utterly invincible. Ademir, Jair, and Zizinho were all sensational. Fans across the country were giddy with anticipation. Brazil was closer than ever to capturing that coveted first World Cup. The other team in the Final Pool, Uruguay, was just trying to keep its head above water. They had reached this stage of the tournament by beating Bolivia—the only other team in its odd two-country grouping—by a score of 8-0. Now they faced Spain and Sweden. The Uruguayans managed a 2-2 tie with the Spaniards, and narrowly beat the Swedes, 3-2. This set up a "final" against Brazil, which had defeated the same two clubs by a total score of 13-2.

Because Brazil had two wins and Uruguay a win and a tie, Brazil only needed to tie Uruguay to win the World Cup. Obviously, Uruguay needed to beat Brazil. Under these unusual circumstances, Brazil could have collapsed into a defensive shell for 90 minutes and walked away with the championship. But that wasn't about to happen. The confident Brazilians, driven by the ceaseless, deafening roar of more than 200,000 of their fans, meant to dismantle Uruguay and prove their soccer supremacy.

Prior to the game, Uruguayan soccer officials congratulated the team on making it so far, and announced that if they could keep the score respectable (4-0 was specifically mentioned) then a loss would still be considered an outstanding achievement. With friends like that, who needs enemies?

Perhaps that very thought was going through the mind of Uruguay's keeper, Maspoli, as he turned away shot after shot in the first half. The Brazilian attack was relentless. Ademir, already with seven goals to his credit, was all over the field. Zizinho and Jair were a half-step behind. You could practically see the adrenaline pumping through the Brazilian team, as they skittered back and forth and beat Uruguay to almost every loose ball. There was just one problem: whatever they tried, they could not score. Varela and Andrade were participating beautifully, making the Brazilian forwards work hard for their shots and helping Maspoli cut down the angles. When the whistle blew to end the first half, the score stood, 0-0.

During the intermission, Brazilian fans reminded one another that a scoreless tie was as good as a win. But deep down they knew this was not true. In the locker room, the players knew this, too. No one wanted to win a World Cup by tying Uruguay.

When play resumed, Brazil still had its high-octane offensive going. This time it was too much for Uruguay, as Alcides Friaca spotted an opening two minutes into the period and drove the ball into the back of the net. Maracana erupted in celebration. The Brazilian players were relieved to be on the board. You could see that they were finally feeling good about their games. They felt they could relax now and just soak up the love.

They could not have been more wrong. In their moment of glory, the Brazilians lost their edge and their opponents knew it. For the next 20 minutes, led by the fleet-footed Ghiggia, Uruguay pounded the ball inside and had Brazil backpedaling. Schi-

This postage stamp commemorates the great performance of Uruguay's Alcide Ghiggia in the 1950 final against Brazil.

POWER PLAYER: ADEMIR—BRAZIL

Ademir was a keeper's worst nightmare. He could shoot with power and accuracy equally well with either foot, and seemed to know a goalie's next move before the goalie did. Ademir was the star of Brazil's powerful postwar teams, and nearly delivered the 1950 World Cup to his country. Ademir's offensive prowess (he scored 32 goals in 37 international games) is credited with the creation of the 4-2-4 formation. He was so dangerous from his position at center forward that opponents had to rearrange their lineups to pull back an extra defender. Still, Brazil's World Cup foes were ill-prepared for Ademir in 1950, as he netted seven goals in the tournament.

affino took a pass from Ghiggia and hammered it past Brazil's keeper, Barbosa, to even the score.

It was as if someone pulled the plug on the crowd. There is nothing "louder" than 205,000 people (still the largest soccer crowd in history) who have stopped cheering. Sensing the disappointment and nervousness of their fans, Brazil's players began playing tentatively. The offense could not regain its killer instinct and the defense began to crumble. Schiaffino was pulled down in the penalty area, but no foul was called. Undaunted, Uruguay continued its pressure. Minutes later, Ghiggia noticed the defense badly out of position in front of Barbosa. He collected a loose ball and sprinted to the outside. The Brazilian defenders, realizing their mistake darted back into position, but Barbosa had to leave a small area exposed. Ghiggia's shot was perfect, curling just inside the post and snapping the net. Uruguay led, 2-1.

The goal completely deflated the Brazilians. They could muster no response, and Uruguay won its second World Cup in as

As this Uruguayan postage stamp shows, the country's performance in the 1950 World Cup generated tremendous national pride.

THE MIRACLE NOBODY KNOWS

Ask soccer fans outside the United States what they consider to be the sport's most incredible upset, and they will be nearly unanimous in their answer: 1950, U.S., 1, England, 0. Ask soccer fans in America about the game, and they just scratch their heads.

The Americans entered the game like lambs being led to slaughter. The players admitted later they did not expect to score, and hoped they could hold their opponents to five goals or less. The match against the Americans was supposed to be a tune-up for England on its way to what everyone believed would be a showdown with Brazil. To get an idea of the disparity between the two clubs, no American had ever received more than $25 to play in a soccer game. The English players—all highly paid professionals—were insured against injury by Lloyd's of London for the then-astounding sum of $3 million!

The game's lone goal, long forgotten more than a half-century later, started with a throw-in by Ed McIlenny on the right sideline, approximately 100 feet from the goal. Halfback Walter Bahr controlled the ball and dribbled in another 10 yards or so. Still working the right side, he looked up and spotted an opening at the far left post. Bahr drove a low shot at medium speed toward the corner, but keeper Bert Williams had it all the way. He moved across the goal line to catch it when Joe Gaetjens, the Haitian-born dishwasher from Brooklyn, slid over from the left.

With the ball coming straight toward his face, Gaetjens cocked his head ever so slightly and it glanced off the side. The misdirection fooled Williams enough so that he could not stop his momentum, and the ball went past him into the net. To this day, the English players wonder whether this was an intentional header, or whether Gaetjens was actually trying to get out of the way. The American players insist that this was their star's "specialty," and that he had done it many times in practice.

The U.S. made the goal stand up, surviving several close calls. The key play came on a hard tackle with 20 minutes left in the second half. Charles Colombo brought down the sharpshooting Mortensen in front of the American net with a body block to the back of the knees. Despite protests from the Brits, the referee ruled that the tackle had been made just outside the penalty area. That meant a free kick instead of a penalty shot. England failed to score, and the game ended, 1-0.

When the final whistle blew, the Brazilian fans raced onto the field and hoisted the American players onto their shoulders. American fans have yet to pay tribute to their national team in this way.

The site of the game, Belo Horizonte, translates to "beautiful horizon." Sadly, there was little on the horizon for U.S. soccer except neglect and obscurity. The sport bungled its chance to build on this amazing victory, and remained a sideshow for decades to come. The next time Team USA appeared in a World Cup match was 1990!

many attempts. It seemed only fitting that, in a tournament of colossal upsets, the final proved to be the greatest one of all. Brazil's disillusioned fans drifted out of Maracana, too distraught to watch Jules Rimet present the trophy to Varela and his teammates. The only sounds that filled the empty stadium were shouts of celebration from the Uruguayan players and the handful of countrymen who had been brave enough to sit in the stands.

> **Winner: Uruguay**
> Runner-up: Brazil
> Best Player: Alcide Ghiggia

1954 Switzerland

The World Cup has never had a "guaranteed" winner going into the tournament. There have been dozens of great teams and hundreds of terrific players, but never has a group of players stood so far above the rest that it seemed impossible that they could be beaten. The closest the tournament ever came was in 1954, when Hungary's "Magic Magyars" rolled into Switzerland undefeated since 1950.

No one questioned the claim that Hungary was the best squad in the world. With stars like Ferenc Puskas, Sandor Kocsis, and Zoltan Czibor, the team played the game better, smarter, and faster than anyone else. Their stiffest competition was expected to come courtesy of England. But in a home-and-home series, Hungary destroyed the Brits 6-3 at Wembley Stadium (the first-ever defeat for an English international team there) and then finished them

Hungary's Ferenc Puskas is captured on the cover of World Sports magazine powering past a helpless defender. Puskas was perhaps the world's top player heading into the 1954 World Cup.

off in Budapest by an even greater margin a few days later.

Puskas and friends would perform against the backdrop of FIFA's 50th anniversary celebration. Switzerland was chosen because it was the home of FIFA's headquarters; Jules Rimet, in his final year as president, could think of no better venue for World Cup 54.

The primary challengers to Hungary's apparent supremacy included Uruguay, Brazil, and West Germany. Uruguay had never been defeated in World Cup play. The defending champions still had Victor Andrade, captain Obdulio Valera, and Juan

Juan Schiaffino, who starred in two World Cups for Uruguay. Among the countless honors he received was his own commemorative postage stamp.

Schiaffino, plus dashing newcomer Jose Santamaria. However, the team seemed less talented overall than in 1950. Brazil, the other finalist in 1950, fielded a team that was almost completely different from the one that faced Uruguay in that final. No one knew what to expect from them, other than speedy, creative, and occasionally out-of-control soccer.

West Germany was an interesting team. Captain Fritz Walter was as tough as they came, forward Helmut Rahn possessed a deadly scoring touch, and Max Morlock was a wonderfully opportunistic player. But the real edge they brought into play was the man working the sideline, Sepp Herberger. The crafty coach had learned a thing or two in the 16 years since he last guided this team in the tournament. And obviously it was a relief not to have Adolf Hitler looking over his shoulder anymore. Indeed, when Herberger saw that both his and Hungary's team had been placed in the same opening-round grouping, he determined that his best chance to take the cup from the Magyars

was to lose to them in their first meeting. Sixteen years earlier that would not have been an option.

The two powerhouses shared Pool 2 with weak squads from Turkey and Korea. Herberger reasoned that he could beat these two clubs with ease, and so West Germany was guaranteed to advance regardless of what transpired in its match with Hungary. Thus when they played, Herberger rested all of his key players and Hungary killed them, 8-3. During the game, West German defender Werner Liebrich fouled Puskas with a hard kick to the ankle. The injury, which many felt was delivered intentionally, dogged him the rest of the tournament. As expected, the Germans then advanced by beating Turkey, 7-2.

In the other groups, play was far more interesting, with plenty of goals to keep the fans on the edge of their seats. Mismatches accounted for many of the high scores, but

West German captain Fritz Walter holds the World Cup trophy as his team poses for a post-game photo.

some games were just good old-fashioned blowouts. The Swiss scored four goals against Italy's normally tough defense. Scotland, sending its first team to the World Cup, fell victim to Uruguay in a 7-0 rout. And Brazil exploded for five goals in a shutout of Mexico. In an exciting tie, England and Belgium combined for eight goals.

The most noteworthy match of the first round was actually a low-scoring affair between France and Yugoslavia. The 1-0 win by the Yugoslavians was the first World Cup game ever to be televised. The broadcast signalled a new era for the tournament, as live coverage of the event would soon begin attracting millions of new fans. It also opened the door to a world of marketing possibilities that would eventually turn the World Cup into a huge money-maker.

In 1954, however, the main focus was still on soccer. In the quarterfinals the scoring barrage continued. Uruguay sent England packing with a 4-2 victory, while Switzerland and Austria squared off in a real barn-burner. The Swiss seized control early with three goals, but the Austrians scored three in seven minutes to even things up. Austria missed a penalty kick, but prevailed nonetheless by a score of 7-5 to put their hosts out of the running. West Germany won in less dramatic fashion over Yugoslavia, 2-0.

The key quarterfinal match pitted Hungary against Brazil. In what came to be known as the "Battle of Berne," the game deteriorated into one of the ugliest spectacles in World Cup history. With the injured Puskas unable to play, the Brazilians smelled blood and primed themselves for an upset. Their strategy was to take the Hungarians off their game with rough-and-tumble tactics. Hungary, anticipating this

strategy, was ready to dish out as much punishment as it absorbed. This put the referee in a difficult spot from the opening kickoff, as players banged into each other, and kicked one another on almost every play. Hungary's Jozsef Bozsik and Brazil's Nilton Santos and Humberto Tozzi were all ejected, and Hungary won the brutal affair by a score of 4-2.

Things actually got worse after the final whistle blew. Following the match, a brawl ensued outside the locker rooms. Hungary's coach, Gustav Sebes, was punched in the face. Puskas joined the fray, and broke a bottle over the head of Pinheiro, the Brazilian captain. It took a cadre of Swiss cops to break up the melee. This was definitely not what Rimet had in mind for FIFA's showcase event.

Hungary had little time to recover from its war with Brazil. Up next in the semifinals was Uruguay, the team Sebes considered the most dangerous in the draw. Puskas would sit this one out, still nursing a sore ankle. But Uruguay's captain, Valera, was out, too. Complicating matters for both teams was the downpour that soaked the field the morning of the game.

Both teams negotiated this quagmire with surprising ease in the early going. The Hungarians struck first on a beautiful bit of teamwork. Nandor Hidegkuti lofted a long pass downfield that Kocsis redirected to the feet of Czibor, who finished the play with a perfect shot. Up 1-0, Hungary pressed its advantage, but couldn't find the back of the net again before intermission. That changed at the start of the second half, as Hidegkuti put his team ahead, 2-0. The goal shook Uruguay from its slumber. Andrade, Schiaffino, Santamaria, and Juan Hohberg launched one attack after another on the

Hungarian keeper Gyula Grosics launches his body at West German forward Hans Schaefer in action from the 1954 final.

gave everyone a chance to catch their breath. When play resumed, Hungary had the upper hand, and Kocsis tallied one goal, then another. Hungary won 4-2, but it was an exhausting victory.

This development, of course, fit right into Sepp Herberger's grand design. West Germany cruised through its semifinal match when the Austrians started backup goalie Walter Zeman to "shake things up." Zeman was the one who was shaking, though, as he was peppered with shots in a 6-1 defeat. Relaxed, well-rested and supremely confident, the Germans were ready to stage the upset Brazil could not.

Herberger felt he had his opponents right where he wanted them. The Magyars had gained nothing in the way of useful information from their earlier encounter. And thanks to the pesky South American clubs, now they were tired and injured. Puskas, still hobbled, talked his way back into the lineup. This was seen as another advantage by the Germans—they felt Puskas at half speed would do more harm than good to Hungary's precision attack.

How wrong they were! Playing on a sloppy, slippery field, the limping superstar found it easy to keep up with everyone else. Six minutes into the game he blasted a ball into the net for a 1-0 lead. Czibor followed with another to make it 2-0. Herberger told his players to keep up the pace. Despite being down two goals, he knew his team could wear Hungary out. The first break for West Germany came on a bit of miscommunication between the Hungarian fullbacks. When neither moved to control a loose ball, Morlock scored to cut the lead in half. Seven minutes later Rahn uncorked a powerful kick that tied the match at 2-2. The Hungarians fought back with two good

Hungarian goal, and just missed with a couple of sizzling shots. With 15 minutes left, Hohberg, on a perfect feed from Schiaffino, scored to cut the deficit in half. Moments later he tied the game with another goal. In the celebration, Hohberg's teammates knocked him unconscious!

The dumfounded Hungarians now found themselves embroiled in an unexpected overtime battle. Uruguay appeared to seize the early advantage, but goalkeeper Gyula Grosics made a stupendous save on the red-hot Hohberg (who regained his senses) to keep Hungary in the match. Andrade went down with an injury, which

POWER PLAYER:
HELMUT RAHN—WEST GERMANY

In his prime, Helmut Rahn ruled the right side of the soccer field. Swooping in from the outside, the tall, heavily built star with the booming right foot terrorized defenses throughout the 1950s, and was the most-watched player in West German football. His tying and winning goals in the 1954 final rank among the supreme individual accomplishments in World Cup play, yet they were only the most memorable moments from a great start-to-finish performance by Rahn at the tournament.

The funny thing is that he almost decided not to play that year. During a tour of South America with his professional team, Rahn entered into negotiations with the Nacional Club of Uruguay. Only a desperate telegram from coach Sepp Herberger convinced him to return.

1954 World Cup hero Helmut Rahn. His trading cards are cherished by collectors the world over.

West Germany's Fritz Walter accepts the World Cup trophy from Jules Rimet after defeating Hungary in the final, 3-2.

scoring opportunities, but Hidegkuti and Kocsis were denied by goal-keeper Anton Turek.

The game became a defensive struggle in the second half, as Herberger was content to wait for Hungary to wear down further. The Germans survived a couple of close calls thanks to sparkling saves by Turek. These seemed to sap the last bit of energy out of the suddenly not-so-Magic Magyars. Finally, Rahn saw his chance, rushed the net, and scored the go-ahead goal. To Puskas's credit, he was the last man on his team to give up. He pushed beyond the pain and made one last gallant charge.

With the crowd on its feet he raced past the German fullbacks and powered a ball past Turek for the apparent game-tying goal. Alas, the referee's whistle had blown; Puskas was offsides.

The final was an upset to be sure, and most definitely reflected a masterful bit of coaching. But in the end it just went to prove that no one is unbeatable in the World Cup, regardless of how well a team plays outside the tournament. After the match, Rimet proudly presented the trophy named after him to Herberger and his players. It was his last official act as president of FIFA.

> **Winner: West Germany**
> **Runner-up: Hungary**
> **Best Player: Helmut Rahn**

1958
Sweden

Every so often an event comes along that sweeps a sport away and deposits it far into the future. Like a mighty river, World Cup 58 picked soccer up and plunked it downstream at a point many historians consider to be the start of the modern era. The "river" in this case was actually a confluence of forces that were already flowing through the game. One was fully expected, the other was a complete revelation.

The one everyone saw coming was television. For the first time, the World Cup would be broadcast around the world. In addition to the TV people, there were 60 international radio crews, and another 1,500 journalists covering the matches.

The one nobody saw coming was a Brazilian teenager named Edson Arantes do Nascimento, but better known as Pele. He was Babe Ruth, Michael Jordan, and Tiger Woods all rolled into one skinny little body. This 17-year-old played a different game than anyone else. For the sport's breakthrough player to "arrive" during the first televised World Cup was a stroke of incredible good fortune, and paved the way for soccer to eventually flourish even in the most remote corners of the world.

Pele demonstrated a level of expertise and artistry that no one had ever seen and few had dared to imagined. His instincts were sublime, and his physical tools just as fine. Pele was the perfect player. The most amazing thing about him in 1958, however, is that almost no one knew who he was. Even Brazil's coach did not fully understand the talent he possessed. Incredibly, Vincent Feola planned to keep Pele on the bench!

In Feola's defense, his veterans were all exceptional players, particularly Nilton Santos and captain Luis Bellini. Until he saw a good reason to do otherwise, he planned to keep them on the field as much as possible. He may also have been swayed by the main criticism of the national team: Brazil pushed its young players too hard and expected too much. Time and again they failed in international competition, disintegrating into crazy, undisciplined play, and inexperience was seen as the main cause. For World Cup 58 the team actually brought its own traveling psychologist to work with the players and prevent them from being overwhelmed. Meanwhile, Feola had devised a 4-2-4 alignment that gave his team great flexibility and made the transition from defense to offense and back lightning-fast. However, it also enabled opponents to control the center of the field.

The most-watched team heading into the tournament was England. The previous winter, a plane crash had taken the lives of several top players, including Tommy Taylor and Duncan Edwards, who was one of the game's rising stars. The national team rallied in honor of their fallen mates, but the lost talent could not easily be replaced. A 5-0 loss to Yugoslavia in a "pre-Cup" exhibition match seemed to confirm this fact.

Normally, the Hungarians would have been among the favorites, but they were undermanned as well. Three of their stars—Ferenc Puskas, Zoltan Czibor, and Sandor Kocsis—decided not to return to Communist Hungary after a South American tour and defected. West Germany, always a solid team, was getting a bit thick around the middle. Its stars were aging, and no young players had stepped forward to take their places. Coach Sepp Herberger still relied heavily on his 38-year-old captain Fritz Walter, while Helmut Rahn—once a potent goal-scorer—had ballooned out of shape.

Some said the Soviets had the best team. They certainly had the best goalie. Young Lev Yashin was the best keeper of his generation, and perhaps the best ever. The gritty Igor Netto was the team's top international star. Because all Russian players were technically amateurs, the USSR played a lot of soccer against non-professionals. No one could say for sure how they would perform against the best pros in the world.

Sweden had a respectable squad thanks to Lennart Skoglund, Nils Liedholm, and Kurt Hamrin, who were respected players in the European pro leagues. But besides being the host country, the Swedes had little else going for them, including their own fans. The people had purchased their tickets to see the other teams, not their own. The Swedish federation, in fact, ended up having to hire cheerleaders to get people revved up.

Brazil made an early statement by trouncing Austria, 3-0. The players watching from Feola's bench, however, were probably better than the ones on the field. On the sidelines were young stars Pele, Vava, Zito, and Garrincha. And with the exception of Vava that is where they stayed during the next match, against England. When the game ended in a scoreless tie, Feola could sense increased tension in the locker room, and knew he might have to shake things up to keep his players focused.

Lev Yashin shows why opponents called him "The Octopus." The acrobatic Russian goalkeeper gave the Soviet Union a chance to win any game it played.

The team's veteran leaders actually came up with the solution. They met with Feola prior to Brazil's game against the USSR and asked that the kids be inserted in the lineup. The coach agreed and the results were magical. The Soviets found themselves in the middle of a hornets' nest. Moments after kickoff Garrincha rattled the post with a blistering shot. Two minutes later Vava took a gorgeous pass from Didi, and booted it past Yashin for a 1-0 lead. He added another later in the match to seal a 2-0 victory for the Brazilians, who cruised into the next round. Afterwards, Russian coach Gabriel Katchalin said he had never seen such a beautiful brand of soccer.

The second team out of this group was decided by a playoff between the USSR and England. Yashin stymied the English scorers with his second shutout of the tournament and the Russians advanced to the quarterfinals. The other quarterfinalists included some surprises, including Sweden, Wales, and France, which captivated the crowd with its run-and-gun style. The French netted 11 goals in three games, with forward Just Fontaine doing most of the damage on feeds from Raymond Kopa. Noticeable by their absence were the Hungarians, who lost without their big stars.

France continued to roll in the next round, walloping Northern Ireland on goals by Fontaine and Kopa. Their next opponent was Brazil, which got to the semis with a 1-0 victory over Wales. It had been the kind of game that always seemed to trip up Brazil in the past. The Welsh players were disciplined, tough, and strong; the match was a struggle from start to finish. But Brazil played mistake-free soccer and kept their scoreless streak alive in an impressive

1-0 win. The lone goal came off the foot of Pele, who was just beginning to make his presence felt.

Much to the surprise of their fans, the Swedish players survived their quarterfinal meeting with Yashin and the Russians. The keeper turned in another scintillating performance under a constant barrage of shots, but let in two goals while his teammates scored none. The West Germans, meanwhile, got a goal from Rahn and made it stand up against Yugoslavia for a 1-0 victory.

In the Sweden-West Germany semifinal, the home fans finally got into it and began to make themselves heard. They were soon quieted, however, when Hans Schafer scored from 25 yards out—then reenergized by Skoglund 10 minutes later when he knotted the game with a controversial goal. Prior to his shot, teammate Liedholm touched the ball with his hand. The referee did not see it, however, so the goal counted. The Swedes quickly gained an emotional edge, and pressed the West Germans the rest of the way. When Ernst Juskowiak was ejected in the second half, West Germany was forced to play a man short. Sweden took full advantage, as Hamrin and Gunnar Gren scored minutes before regulation time expired. For the first time in history, the Swedes were going to the final.

In the other semifinal, Brazil played the over-aggressive Frenchmen like a Stradivarius. Pele and his teammates counter-attacked whenever possible and capitalized on every defensive lapse. Vava opened the scoring with a goal for Brazil, but Fontaine tied matters with one of his own nine minutes later. Late in the half, Didi made it 2-1 with a goal that gave his team momentum heading into the locker room. The second half was a clinic, as Pele scored three times in a 23-minute span to send the French reeling. The final score was 5-2. After the game, goal-keeper Claude Abbes said, "I would rather play against 10 Germans than one Brazilian."

Brazil rightfully went into the final as the overwhelming favorite. Swedish coach George Rayner was one of many who acknowledged that his team was older and slower than Brazil's. Their only hope was that Brazil would revert to old habits and play stupid, sloppy soccer in a big game. This possibility seemed very real when Sweden got the game's first goal on a shot by Liedholm.

In past years, the Brazilians would have looked at each other accusingly, and then panicked. But these young guns were fearless and focused. Instead of being fractured by this setback, Brazil came together as a team. Garrincha raced down the right side minutes later, darted past two Swedish defenders, then sent a hard pass across the goal mouth that Vava redirected into the net. The same two hooked up again later in the first half to put their team ahead, 2-1. Brazil was now firing on all cylinders, controlling every phase of the game.

The Brazilians picked up where they left off to start the second half. In the 55th minute, Pele left fans around the world rubbing their eyes in disbelief when he scored his team's third goal. Taking a high pass with his back to the goal, he volleyed the ball into the air, then spun his body up and over as if to do a backflip. With his head pointing down and his feet pointing up, Pele struck the ball as he spun completely around and blistered a shot into the Swedish goal. It was the most awesome move a soccer player had ever tried, and it resulted in a goal during the World Cup final, on world-

Pele watches as Sweden's Kalle Svensson dives in a futile attempt to stop his shot. It was one of two goals he scored in the final.

A proud and exhausted Brazilian team poses after winning the 1958 final. The teenage sensation Pele is squatting, third from left.

wide television. The crowd was agog. The Swedish players had no idea how to react. Even Pele's own teammates weren't entirely sure what they had just seen. With the fans still buzzing, Brazil closed out the match with two more goals, including a less-spectacular one by Pele.

The Brazilians celebrated their 5-2 win with untethered joy. After years of frustration and criticism, they were champions—the first to win the World Cup on another continent. They galloped around waving their flag, then took up Sweden's flag to honor their opponents. The Swedish fans cheered approvingly, knowing that no one could have beaten Brazil on this day. And, sensing, perhaps, that soccer would never be quite the same again.

Winner: Brazil
Runner-up: Sweden
Best Player: Pele

1962
Chile

FIFA was not in the habit of switching World Cup venues. Once a host country was selected, that was that. However, there could always be an exception. Two years before World Cup 62, as Chile was just beginning to gear up for the tournament it had been awarded several years earlier, the nation was rocked by a killer earthquake, then suffered through a horrendous drought. Although the Chilean people did not lose their spirit, the country itself was a mess. No one was sure how this would effect the World Cup, but Argentina stepped in and offered to host just in case. Carlo Dittburn, president of the Chilean Football Federation, insisted his country could handle the flow of fans, and looked forward to the positive impact the World Cup would have on his country's economy.

FIFA decided to stick with Chile, on the strength of Dittburn's promises as much as anything else. When he died a month prior to the tournament, the nation went into mourning, and named the new soccer stadium in Arica in his honor. The national team also seemed transformed by Dittburn's death. Riding a wave of emotion and playing at home in front of wildly supportive crowds, the players were poised to reach a whole new level.

They would have far to go to challenge the supremacy of Brazil, the overwhelming favorite in this tournament. Though illness forced coach Vicente Feola to step down, Aimore Moreira proved a suitable replacement. He knew the players, the players knew him, and his brother had run the national squad in the mid 1950s. Given Brazil's lineup, coaching wasn't much of a concern, anyway. The team was loaded with stars, including Pele, who was just coming into his full glory at age 21. Garrincha, Zito, and Vava were also among the world's top ten players, and a young player named Amarildo seemed destined for greatness, too. The only concern for Brazil was the fitness of veterans Djalma and Nilton Santos.

Spain also appeared to be playing with a stacked deck. Thanks to the efforts of the country's top pro club, Real Madrid, Spain had recruited and then naturalized several top players in time to add them to the national team. Ferenc Puskas of Hungary, Alfredo di Stefano of Argentina, and Jose Santamaria of Uruguay were now Spanish citizens. Puskas and di Stefano, once the two best players in Europe, were no longer in their prime, so it was hard to say just how good the Spaniards were.

Italy, which still had old political and economic ties to the South American nations of Brazil and Argentina, made the most of these relationships by naturalizing a quartet of stars for their World Cup team.

Jose Altafini and Angelo Sormani both hailed from Brazil, while Omar Sivori and Kumberto Maschio were born in Argentina. These players bolstered a nucleus of talented youngsters that made Italy a threat to win any game it played.

Also in the mix for World Cup 62 were the USSR and Czechoslovakia. Each team had a great goalie. The Soviets' Lev Yashin, had become the best keeper in the world. Right behind him was Wilhelm Schroiff, who had a reputation for making big saves in big situations. Another team from Eastern Europe that had a chance was Yugoslavia. The Yugos were powered by Dragan Sekularac, a temperamental forward with an explosive goal-scoring touch.

Although the games were exciting, the first round offered little in the way of surprises. The USSR proved the class of Group 1, after beating Yugoslavia and Uruguay. Yashin was not in top form, however, as he allowed four goals in a draw with Colombia. Yugoslavia also advanced from this group.

Brazil beat Mexico 2-0 in its first match, but at great cost. Pele tore his hamstring in the game and was lost for the tournament. A scoreless tie with Czechoslovakia followed, as Moreira's team struggled to adjust. But even without their best player, the Brazilians still looked tough. In their third game, a showdown with Spain, Amarildo stepped up with a pair of second-half goals to turn a 1-0 deficit into a 2-1 victory. The Spaniards, who had lost di Stefano to an injury, failed to advance.

Amarildo's inspiring performance should have been the talk of the tournament, but it was overshadowed by the commotion surrounding the Italy-Chile match. Weeks earlier, Italian newspapers ran sensational stories about the wretched conditions in Chile. They painted a vivid picture of illiteracy, alcoholism, and other social ills that shocked Europeans who were unaware of Chile's plight. The Chilean media responded by writing "exposes" on the Italian players. They also reminded soccer fans that the only reason Italy had a chance was because of the South Americans they had "stolen" for their team. By the time the two countries played, the game was being called the "Battle of Santiago."

As the Italians walked onto the field, they tried to win over the fans by tossing roses into the crowd. This gesture was met by taunts and insults, and the flowers were thrown back at them. The game itself was rough from the beginning, and got progressively worse. Players kicked each other as often as they kicked the ball, and spit in each other's faces. Italy's Giorgio Ferrini was ejected just minutes into the contest for rough tackling, but when Chile's Leonel Sanchez (the son of a boxer) flattened Maschio and broke his nose with a right cross, he was allowed to stay in the game. The referee, perhaps fearing for his own safety, "missed" this incident and ordered everyone to play on. After a scoreless first half, Italy's Mario David and Chile's Ferrini had to be separated under the stands.

With the field officials still favoring them, the Chilean players finally broke through in the second half and scored twice to win the game. The referee admitted later that he had wanted to suspend the game after 45 minutes, but believed that this would have caused a riot.

The victory helped Chile advance, and set up a quarterfinal match against the Soviet Union. Yashin played poorly, allowing two long shots to elude him. Chile let in just one goal to pull off a huge upset and move on to the semifinals. Yugoslavia also made it to the semis, defeating West Germany 1-0 on a late goal by Deter Radakovic. The Czechs defeated Hungary by the same score thanks to the stellar work of their keeper, Schroiff, who turned back the Hungarian offense time and again. The other quarterfinal featured a 3-1 wipeout of England by Brazil. Garrincha dominated play, with a pair of goals and a lovely assist. The team was coming together nicely, despite the absence of Pele.

Due to a scheduling quirk, the two semifinals were held on the same day, at the same time, in different locations. The stadium in Arica was filled past capacity for the Brazil-Chile match, while only 5,000 showed up to watch Yugoslavia and Czechoslovakia. The smaller crowd saw the better game, as Schroiff played magnificently again. He made several spectacular saves in a 3-1 victory that sent the Czech team to the final for the first time since 1934.

In the other semifinal, Chile was in way over its head. The only hope for the home team was to disrupt Brazil's flow with the same rough tactics it had employed against Italy. To their credit, the Brazilians did not get tricked into a boxing match, and simply played through the pain. Garrincha was unstoppable, netting two goals in the first half. Chile scored after intermission, sending the crowd into a frenzy. But Vava came though with two goals to seal a 4-2 win. Brazil was now within one victory of a second straight championship.

With the game in hand and just a few minutes left, Garrincha finally decided enough was enough and traded punches with one of his opponents. The referee sent him off the field, and Garrincha was showered with debris from the stands, including a glass bottle which hit him in the head and opened a sizable gash. FIFA officials debated whether to suspend the star for the final. Brazil's President, Tancredo Neves, tried to intervene on Garrincha's behalf, sending a telegram to the association's disciplinary committee. No one can say for certain whether his words carried any weight, but a day later FIFA president, Sir Stanley Rous, made the somewhat surprising announcement that Garrincha would play.

The experts were unmoved by this development. In their opinion, it made little difference to Czechoslovakia. Regardless of the players they faced, the team would stick with what worked: a conservative attack led by their top scorer, Josef Masopust, backed up by a tight defense and the goaltending of Schroiff.

Hoping to catch Brazil by surprise, Czech coach Rudolf Vytlacil fooled the experts and instructed his players to attack the Brazilian goal with uncharacteristic abandon. He knew this would leave Schroiff open to a counterattack, but was banking that his keeper could continue making great saves. When Masopust scored in the 16th minute, Vytlacil was looking pretty smart. Brazil bounced back, however, and began to gain the upper hand. Amarildo scored on a severe angle, squeezing a shot between Schroiff and the post. The game went into intermission knotted at 1-1, but the Czech goalie's aura of invincibility had been shattered.

In the second half Amarildo struck again, this time with a beautiful cross to

Brazilian halfback Zito celebrates the deciding goal of the 1962 final. He was all over the field against Czechoslovakia.

Zito. All by himself in front of the net, the Brazilian calmly headed home the goal that gave his team the lead. This play further unnerved Schroiff and his teammates. Minutes later Djalma scooped a soft, arching shot towards the Czech goal-keeper. With the sun in his eyes, Schroiff struggled to catch the high lob. When he lost control of the ball, Vava was there to tap it in. That finished the scoring for the day, as Brazil held on for a 3-1 victory. The country joined Italy and Uruguay as two-time World Cup champs.

Even minus Pele, Brazil showed it was still the best. Despite the fact that many of its stars were in their 30s, the team's ability to dribble, pass, shoot, and defend remained as fresh and vibrant as ever. With a new wave of players on the horizon and Pele in his prime, Brazil seemed on the verge of a soccer dynasty.

> **Winner: Brazil**
> **Runner-up: Czechoslovakia**
> **Best Player: Garrincha**

1966 England

Ask any British citizen where soccer was invented, and you'll get the answer "England!" every time. That's why the country was so proud to be the World Cup host in 1966. This was more than 100 years after the English had given birth to the Football Association,

POWER PLAYER: GARRINCHA—BRAZIL

The most accomplished dribbler and passer in World Cup history was the "Little Bird," Brazil's Garrincha. While overcoming childhood polio, he fantasized about playing soccer for hours on end, dreaming up incredible plays and making impossible passes in his mind. When he returned to health, he could hardly wait to get on the field. Garrincha's slightly twisted legs gave him an odd advantage which neither he nor anyone else has ever fully explained.

Operating from the right wing, he was a magician with the ball. Garrincha was a great asset in other ways. He liked to keep his teammates loose with a sly sense of humor and elaborate practical jokes. Ironically, this nearly cost him a spot on the 1958 World Cup team. Coach Vincente Feola, worried that his players would be distracted by their strange surroundings, decided to leave the disruptive Garrincha back home in Rio. The players claimed the opposite was true, and convinced Feola to reinstate the 24-year-old.

Garrincha proved in 1958, and again in 1962, that he was the most imaginative playmaker in the world. Over the years he proved his value to his team again and again. Without him, Brazil might still have won in 1958. But the team would not have had a chance four years later after losing Pele in the opening round.

An older, wiser Pele prior to his third World Cup. The Brazilian superstar was the target of rough tactics by opponents.

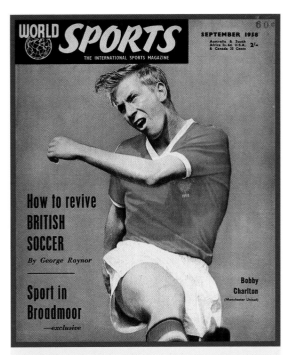

Bobby Charlton graces the cover of World Sports. His international fame made him one of soccer's most marketable stars.

the first organization to clearly differentiate between rugby and soccer. Yet for all their history and know how, the English had never enjoyed much success in the World Cup. They hoped to change their fortunes in 1966.

There was good reason to believe that this might be the year it would happen. Since being named England's coach three years earlier, Alf Ramsey had boldly maintained that his team would win the Jules Rimet trophy. To that end, he schooled his players in strategies developed exclusively for World Cup play. Ramsey concocted a new defensive-minded alignment that called for his wings to drop back from the front line and help the fullbacks whenever

possible. In turn, England became a versatile squad that could adjust rapidly on defense while still striking quickly and efficiently on offense.

England's leader on the field was defensive wizard, Bobby Moore. Behind him was the tough and resourceful goal-keeper, Gordon Banks. The team's offensive punch was provided by Bobby Charlton—considered one of the 10 best players in history—along with Alan Ball, Roger Hunt, and Jimmy Greaves. Charlton in particular had to be watched at all times. He specialized in burning keepers who cheated too far off their with long, accurate shots. There were several other capable players on the roster, including Geoff Hurst, a late addition by Ramsey. Another reason to like England's chances was its status as host. The players knew all the sounds, smells, and eccentricities of the country's ancient soccer venues, including Wembley Stadium, where the final would be played. Making sure not to take the World Cup too seriously, the Brits had refused to construct new arenas for the tournament.

This "no big deal" attitude caught up with England prior to the opening match, when someone simply walked off with the Jules Rimet trophy, which was on display, unguarded, at a local stamp show. English officials frantically searched for the trophy, but could turn up no solid clues. A dog named Pickles saved the day, when he sniffed out the missing hardware in a garbage heap while on his daily walk.

Thanks to Pickles, the 16 teams who had assembled for the tournament had something to play for. All eyes were on Brazil, the defending two-time champion. Coach Vicente Feola had returned to the sidelines and he welcomed back Gilmar, Djalma Santos, Garrincha, and the incomparable Pele from the 1962 squad. Though Portugal lacked Brazil's depth, it had Eusebio, the most powerful and dynamic player in Europe, and Mario Coluna, a deadly marksman. West Germany, Italy, and the Soviet Union were considered contenders, too. The West Germans, now under the guidance of Helmut Schoen, were particularly dangerous, especially with veteran Uwe Seeler and 21-year-old superstar Franz Beckenbauer in top form.

England opened the tournament cautiously against Uruguay. In a match which offered little excitement, the teams sleepwalked to a scoreless tie. The most noteworthy action came afterwards in the locker room, as players from both sides submitted to the first ever World Cup drug test; from that day on, teams would be checked after every match for substances banned by FIFA.

England found its rhythm and beat its next two opponents, Mexico and France, to advance. Hunt scored three times in these victories, but Greaves hurt his leg against the French and would be out of action for at least a week. Ramsey inserted Hurst in his stead. In Group 2, the West Germans drubbed Switzerland, 5-0. A draw with Argentina, followed by a win over Spain, moved them comfortably into the next

Eusebio shows off his wizardry on the front of a media Fax File card. His marvelous one-man performance in 1966 ranks among the World Cup's greatest stories.

round. Seeler and Beckenbauer played excellent soccer in all three matches.

While Groups 1 and 2 played to form, there were big surprises in the other two brackets. Brazil started smoothly with a 2-0 win over Bulgaria, but Pele was brutalized in the match. He had to sit out the next game, against Hungary, which shocked Brazil 3-1 on the fine play of Florian Albert. Now the Brazilians found themselves in a tough spot. Facing Portugal, they needed a victory to advance. It was not to be. Though Pele played, he wasn't in peak health. Eusebio, meanwhile, was nearly unstoppable for Portugal. Though closely marked, he pumped two goals into the net to give his team the victory. Tending to his wounds afterwards, Pele showed justifiable frustration over the thuggery he had encountered throughout the tournament, and vowed that he would never again compete in a World Cup match.

The story in Group 4 was the amazing run made by North Korea, a team that had made it into the tournament only because 14 African countries had dropped out in protest of FIFA's qualifying process. They were the most dangerous kind of team—one that felt no pressure—and they captivated the British fans with the joyful way they played. With the USSR advancing as expected, the second spot belonged to the winner of the game between North Korea and the powerful Italy. In a closely contested first half, Italy played nervously, which led to a mistake. Pak Doo Ik scooped up a loose ball and fired into the net for a 1-0 lead. Try as they might, the Italians were unable to equalize things in the second half, and were sent packing. When they arrived in Rome, the players were met by fans at the airport and pelted with rotten fruit.

In the quarterfinals, the North Koreans added to their great story by scoring three times in 20 minutes against Portugal. Unfortunately, they had no answer for Eusebio, who led his team to five straight goals and a 5-3 victory. The Soviets won their match against Hungary 2-1 on a wonderful performance by goalie, Lev Yashin. Hungarian keeper Jozef Gelei—one of the world's best—committed two costly errors and both resulted in enemy goals.

The other quarterfinal matches were the subject of suspicion and controversy. The only South American teams left in the draw were Argentina, which played England, and Uruguay, which was scheduled to face West Germany. FIFA assigned an Englishman to referee West Germany-Uruguay, and a German to referee England-Argentina. As if by prearrangement, those officiating seemed to favor the European clubs, while key calls went against the South Americans. Many an eyebrow was raised when Argentina's captain, Antonio Rattin, was ejected for misconduct. His behavior didn't even come close to crossing the line. England won, 1-0. When the Argentine players protested, Ramsey called them "animals" and said they were sore losers. Uruguay had plenty to complain about, too. Two of their best players were sent off by the referee, and they fell to West Germany, 4-0.

The first semifinal pitted West Germany against the Soviet Union. Helmut Haller put the West Germans ahead with a goal just before intermission, then Beckenbauer added another midway through the second half. Though the USSR got one back late in the game, the outcome was never really in doubt. West Germany advanced to the final for the first time since claiming the title in 1954.

The swift and powerful Eusebio prepares to unleash a shot against Hungary. He left the field in tears when Portugal fell to England in the semifinals.

England's semifinal match against Portugal featured thrilling play by both Charlton and Eusebio. The English star opened the scoring in the 30th minute, sending the packed house in Wembley into hysterics. The game score held at 1-0 until late in the second half when Charlton did it again. With his team down 2-0 Eusebio tried to spearhead a desperate rally. He thumped a shot past Banks 10 minutes later, but it was too little, too late. Eusebio walked off the field in tears.

In seven meetings with the Germans since 1936, England had lost six times and tied once. Although the crowd would be on England's side, the "home field" advantage would be lessened by the fact that thousands of Germans had managed to lay their hands on tickets for the match. Alf Ramsey knew his team needed a spark, and he decided to stick with the hot player, Hurst, instead of reinserting Greaves into the lineup. Though well enough to play, the veteran star would be held back until needed.

England began the game playing sloppy soccer and paid for it when Haller intercepted a poor clearing ball and scored on Banks. Later in the first half, Moore booted a long free kick toward the German goal. The defense was slow getting to the ball, allowing the deceptively quick Hurst to slice through and head the ball past a shocked Hans Tilkowski. The English fans erupted in celebration.

The score remained tied deep into the second half. Both teams launched bold offensive attacks, but both Banks and Tilkowski were equal to the challenge. Then, in the 77th minute, England's Martin Peters put his team ahead when he smashed a loose ball into the net. Moments later, Charlton broke into the clear but his shot sailed wide. The West Germans set the their jaws, narrowed their eyes, and mounted one last all-out offensive. Just before the final whistle blew, Wolfgang Weber got his foot on a ball during a scramble in front of Banks and drove it home. For the first time in 32 years, the final would go more than 90 minutes.

Ramsey pleaded with his dispirited troops to stay focused on the task at hand. He assured them that the enemy was tiring. "They're finished!," he screamed. Ten minutes into extra time, Hurst took a cross from Ball, and blasted a shot towards the West German goal. The ball struck the underside of the bar, ricocheted straight down, then spun back out onto the playing field. The English players raised their hands in celebration, certain the shot was a goal. The referee wasn't sure. Had the ball crossed the line? The linesman signalled that it had.

West Germany tried to answer, but England was too strong. When Hurst collected his third goal of the match—becoming the first player to record a hat trick in the final—the scoring was done. England captured its first World Cup by a score of 4-2. The West Germans, though immensely disappointed, acknowledged their opponents as the better team. The English players, meanwhile, carried Moore on their shoulders around Wembley Stadium. In the minds of every right-thinking Brit, the Jules Rimet trophy had finally arrived at its proper resting place.

Wolfgang Weber boots the ball past English goalkeeper Gordon Banks to score the tying goal with seconds left in regulation of the 1966 final. England recovered to win 4-2 in extra time.

POWER PLAYER:
GEOFF HURST—ENGLAND

Though Bobby Moore and Bobby Charlton were the sparkplugs of England's great 1966 World Cup team, Geoff Hurst was the difference-maker. Inserted for Jimmy Greaves after the veteran was injured in the opening match, Hurst was expected to do what he did for his West Ham club in the English league: limit mistakes, blend into the team, and take good shots when he had them.

What everyone hoped he would do was rise to the occasion and make big plays, as he had done so many times in FA Cup competition. Indeed, Hurst was at his best during the English championship playoffs. He scored 23 career goals for West Ham in post-season matches—quite impressive considering he had a grand total of 46 during more than a decade of regular-season play.

Hurst had solid skills and a solid body, but lacked the magnetism of a true star. This worked to his advantage in World Cup 66, because England's opponents sometimes forgot he was even there. What they failed to realize was that he had the kind of explosive speed that comes into play when you least expect it. West Germany all but ignored him in the final and paid the ultimate price—to this day no one other than Hurst has scored a hat trick in the championship game. Still a popular national hero, Hurst was knighted in 1998.

English captain Bobby Moore celebrates on the shoulders of Geoff Hurst and Ray Wilson. Hurst scored the goal that beat West Germany in a thrilling final.

1970
Mexico

After four decades, the World Cup was finally living up to its name. No longer a battle for soccer supremacy between Europe and South America, it was now being contested by 71 countries from all over the globe. Qualifying matches started in 1968, fueling worldwide interest long before the games began. This would be the first World Cup televised in full color, which added to the excitement and also spurred global sales of color TVs. As host of this groundbreaking event, Mexico turned its 114,000-seat Stadia Azteca into a soccer showplace.

To ensure that European fans could watch live matches, many were scheduled during daylight hours. This meant Mexico City's high altitude and summer sun would come into play. (Two years earlier, during the 1968 Olympics, athletes had felt winded and hot). Thus endurance and stamina would be among the keys to survival. England was one of many squads to make special preparations for the country's challenging climate. The defending champs arrived in Mexico a full month before their first match to start training. Coach Alf Ramsey went so far as to ship tons of frozen and canned English food to his team's hotel, ensuring that his players would enjoy as many of the comforts of home as possible.

England's squad wasn't much different than the one that took the title in 1966. Bobby Moore again anchored the team, while Gordon Banks patrolled the net as goal-keeper. The offensive punch was provided by the likes of Bobby Charlton, Geoff Hurst, and Alan Ball. Among those hoping to dethrone England were Italy, Peru, and Uruguay. The Italians had become masters of a conservative, defensive style of play that was gaining popularity in international competition. It wasn't that Italy lacked scoring ability; in Gigi Riva and Roberto Boninsegna the team had a pair of talented attackers. But the Italians preferred to wait for their opponent to make mistakes, and were content to rely on goal-keeper Enrico Albertosi to keep them in every match. Peru was dangerous mostly because of its new coach, Didi. The former Brazilian star had transformed the Peruvian players into a real threat, as Argentina discovered to its great embarrassment in a qualifying loss. Uruguay, the 1950 champion, was a contender if for no other reason than it always found a way to play Brazil tough.

The Brazilians were the most fascinating team in this World Cup. No country in the world could field more talented players, yet no country came into World Cup 70 embroiled in as much controversy. The new national coach, Joao Saldanha, had fiddled endlessly with his lineup during the Spring, dropping one star after another from his roster. Saldanha finally went too far when he threatened to get rid of Pele. Saldanha became the most hated man in South America, and soon after this he snapped, showing up at a local club's training camp wielding a gun. Mario Zagallo, a member of Brazil's championship team in 1958 and 1962, was quickly named as his replacement.

Zagallo immediately restored order by patching things up with Pele, reinstating Rivelino, and inserting Tostao, Jairzinho, and Gerson back into their familiar positions. All five were among the Top 20 players in the world, and the new coach was more than happy to let them do their thing. Zagallo also welcomed the contributions of an up-and-coming star named Clodoaldo. If the Brazilians played their best, it would take a monumental effort for anyone else to beat them.

The World Cup opened with Mexico and the USSR playing to a ho-hum tie. What stood out most about the contest was the way referee Kurt Tschenscher called the action. Before the tournament, FIFA had instructed all 30 of its officials to show no tolerance towards dirty play. Such tactics had seriously detracted from 1966 event, almost pushing Pele into early retirement. Thanks to rules put in place by FIFA, referees now had real power at their disposal to clean up the game. A new card system enabled them to communicate with all players, no matter what language they spoke. A yellow card indicated a warning and a red card meant automatic ejection. Tschenscher assessed four yellow cards in the Mexico-USSR match.

Of the four groups in the tournament's opening round, Brazil's was easily the most compelling—mainly because it included England. Many fans believed these two powerhouses would meet in the final, so the thought of a first-round "preview" was very exciting. The match did not disappoint. Both teams came into the game with a win under their belts. Brazil was weakened by the absence of Gerson, out with an injury, but still had plenty of firepower. Early in the first half, Jairzinho sent a beautiful cross to Pele, who jumped high in the air and headed the ball on a line towards the far post. The Brazilian players were actually

Gordon Banks hits the turf after deflecting a header by Pele. The English keeper's miraculous save is still considered one of the greatest plays in World Cup competition.

starting to celebrate when Banks—contorting his airborne body—reached out and somehow batted the shot away. It was the finest save most people had ever seen, and it was seen by countless millions around the world, live and in color.

The match remained a tense, scoreless tie through halftime and up until the 60th minute. This time Pele and Jairzinho worked the same play in reverse, and Banks was helpless to stop it. England pressed its attack through the final 30 minutes but could not score. After the 1-0 victory, Pele swapped jerseys with Moore and exchanged some friendly words. They knew they might face each other again.

The win enabled Brazil to advance, and England followed suit by winning its next match, against Czechoslovakia. The opening-round matches in the other groups, though far less dramatic, went more or less as expected. Peru and Uruguay moved on, as did the Italians, who made the most of their lone goal to earn a victory and two draws.

Italy began to gain a better offensive flow in the quarterfinals with a 4-1 win to eliminate Mexico. Riva scored twice in the game. Brazil also scored four times, while allowing Peru just two scores. Tostao rammed home two goals by himself, and Rivelino and Jairzinho added one each. That put Brazil a win away from the finals, with only the Uruguayans—who had defeated the Soviet Union 1-0—in their way.

The best game of the quarterfinals was the battle between England and West Germany. With Banks suffering from food poisoning, coach Ramsey looked to his backup keeper, Peter Bonetti. Playing with great confidence, the English took a 2-1 lead late into the second half. But the talented sweeper, Franz Beckenbauer, stunned England with a shot that squeezed past Bonetti and sent the match into extra time. With momentum on their side, the Germans resumed their attack, and super scorer Gerd Muller capped the comeback with a magnificent game-winner. The goal was the eighth of the tournament for the man known as "Der Bomber."

In the semifinals, Uruguay surged ahead of Brazil 17 minutes into their contest. The youngster Clodoaldo then knotted the score before the first half ended. Just as Brazil expected, they were being severely tested. With elapsed time now winding down, Jairzinho raced down the right side of the field, cut in towards the middle, and fired a perfect shot that found the back of the net. Rivelino added another goal before the final whistle to make the score 3-1. Brazil was fortunate to have survived.

In the other semifinal, Italy and West Germany clashed in a match for the ages. The Italians seized the early advantage with a goal by Boninsegna, then predictably fell back on defense. The West Germans battered away the rest of the game, but found precious few soft spots. At one point in the second half Beckenbauer made a long dash into the Italian end, only to be walloped by a vicious tackle. He lay on the ground for a time until it was determined he had a dislocated right shoulder. Incredibly, he was back in action a few minutes later with his arm strapped to his chest.

Beckenbauer's grit inspired his teammates. In the 90th minute Karl-Heinz Schnellinger evened the score, sending the match into extra time. That's when things really got interesting. Muller put West Germany ahead, but Tarcisio Burgnich answered back for Italy. Riva then gave the

POWER PLAYER:
PELE—BRAZIL

When Pele exploded onto the world scene in Sweden in 1958, everyone who witnessed his breathtaking performance understood that they were seeing the beginning of a soccer revolution. No one, however, could have guessed how far into the future Pele's impact would reach. After leading Brazil to the championship that year and popularizing the sport in a way no one else ever had, Pele became the most recognized athlete in the world. By the time he led Brazil to a third World Cup win in 1970, he could not walk down the street without being mobbed. This was as true in London or Rome or Moscow or Tokyo as it was in Rio de Janeiro.

The only place Pele remained anonymous was in the United States. Although he enjoyed the peace and quiet he experienced on his trips to the U.S., it frustrated him to see the world's most athletic nation send its best athletes into sports other than soccer.

In the 1970s, Pele made it a point to bring America into the soccer mainstream. He came out of retirement and joined the New York Cosmos of the North American Soccer League, which helped boost soccer's popularity in the U.S. to new heights. After that, Pele began working to bring the World Cup to the United States. In 1994, his dream came true and soccer moved even deeper into the national consciousness. Although little in the way of a tribute was made to Pele during the fine performance of the national team at World Cup 02, anyone who has been following world soccer understands how influential he was in that achievement.

If the "next Pele" comes from an American city or suburb, the superstar's mission will truly be complete.

Pele drills a shot against the Czechs. World Cup 70 was his last for Brazil.

lead to the Italians, but Muller netted another, his tenth of the tournament, to knot the score at 3-3. A minute later Gianni Rivera struck the decisive blow for Italy, sending his team into the final.

Could a talented squad like Brazil's draw Italy out of its defensive shell? This was the question on everyone's mind as the championship game got under way. Some thought Italy might try to surprise Brazil by launching an all-out offensive attack—after all they had scored eight goals in their two previous games. The only sure thing was, as Zagallo gladly confirmed, his players would pounce on every scoring chance they saw and force the Italians to play perfect defense. With Gerson back in the lineup and everyone else healthy, Brazil was considered the favorite.

Italy established from the start that there would be no surprises. The players packed together to form an impenetrable wall. This was just the kind of challenge Pele loved. Though marked closely by the Italian defenders, he shook free when he saw Rivelino winding up to pass the ball. Pele's head and Rivelino's lob came together in front of the Italian net, and Albertosi was helpless to prevent a lovely goal. Twenty minutes later, Italy caught a break when Clodoaldo had a defensive brainlock and enabled Boninsegna to score. Though the match was knotted 1-1 at intermission, Brazil clearly had enjoyed the better play.

This trend continued in the second half. The Italians, slowly withering under Mexico's heat and Brazil's attack, were finding it harder and harder to limit their opponent's scoring chances. Gerson broke the tie with a long shot, then Pele made a little magic when he got a header in front of Albertosi. The entire defense flashed toward the Brazilian superstar when they saw what was

developing, but instead of aiming the ball toward the goal he sent it to a wide-open Jairzinho, who scored. Captain Carlos Alberto finished off the scoring with a hard shot set up, once again, by Pele.

Brazil's 4-1 victory was celebrated by fans throughout the soccer world. The Brazilians demonstrated how beautiful and gripping the sport could be when played at its highest level, and exposed the weaknesses of dull, defensive-minded play. As is the custom in many international sports, Brazil—as three-time champion—retired the Jules Rimet trophy. Just as meaningful to the players were the widespread claims that this 1970 team was the finest to ever set foot on a soccer field.

Italian goalie Enrico Albertosi, #1 is on his knees as Jairzinho, #7 celebrates a lovely goal in the 1970 final. The Brazilian forward scored on a set-up from superstar Pele.

Winner: Brazil
Runner-up: Italy
Best Player: Pele

1974
West Germany

The World Cup came to Germany in 1974, two years after 11 Israeli athletes were killed by Palestinian terrorists at the Olympics in Munich. The tragic events of the 1972 Summer Games made safety for players and fans more important than ever. With everyone still on edge, the Germans had to ensure that nothing of this sort could or would happen again. That required a major expenditure for security.

Cold hard cash, as it turned out, was a running theme throughout World Cup 74. The West German organizing committee predicted the event would generate $40 million. Its mascots—two little boys named Tip and Tap—were auctioned off to sponsors for $2 million. Brazil, despite economic woes, invested $4.5 million in its World Cup team in order to defend its title. Australia, a tournament underdog, offered its player's $4,000 each if they could win a single game. The Dutch players were looking for a little more than that. They threatened to boycott the World Cup if they did not receive hefty pay raises. In the end they were guaranteed at least $24,000 each, plus a cut of Holland's World Cup profits.

Even FIFA got in on the spending spree, unveiling a new prize to replace the Jules Rimet Trophy, which had been retired after Brazil won it for a third time in 1970. The new FIFA World Cup was an impressive piece of hardware. Created by Italian sculp-tor Silvio Gazzanigga, it was fashioned out of gold and cost $20,000.

The Dutch had every reason to expect superstar pay, for they were playing the most entertaining soccer anyone had ever seen. Under coach Rinus Michels, Holland had developed a fluid style that erased many of the distinctions between the different positions. There was a lot of switching and rotating among the players, which created a lot of confusion for opponents. The key to this style was to generate numbers advantages and scoring opportunities. The Dutch called it "Total Soccer," and it depended on highly skilled and creative players, such as Johnny Rep and Johan Neeskens. The team's top player was Johan Cruyff. A

Johan Cruyff waves to the crowd. Along with Johnny Rep (l) and Johan Neeskens (r) he perfected the Dutch style of "Total Soccer."

center-forward, he roamed all over the field, and appeared to have no weaknesses. Many thought he would replace Pele as soccer's next superstar.

Speaking of Pele, he refused to come out of retirement for World Cup 74, despite generous offers from West German organizers to take the field for Brazil. Pele's presence would have increased attendance, television viewership, worldwide interest, and, of course, profits—and would have been a boost to the Brazilian team, which was no longer an offensive juggernaut.

A pair of European countries, Italy and Poland, were installed as favorites along with the hosting West Germans. Italian goal-keeper Dino Zoff was a stone wall; he came into World Cup 74 unbeaten in 11 straight international matches. The Poles, Olympic champs in 1972, were stocked with tough, talented players and had tremendous confidence. Their victory over England in a qualifying match signalled to the sport that Poland was to be taken seriously on the world stage. Indeed, with midfielder Kazimeirz Deyna and wingers Grzegorz Lato and Robert Gadocha providing a powerful offensive punch, this team was a true contender.

West Germany, though minus its top midfielder, Gunter Netzer, had a trio of world-class superstars. Sweeper Franz Beckenbauer was every bit the equal of Cruyff, Gerd Muller was a fearsome scorer, and goal-keeper Sepp Maier made all the stops, even the seemingly impossible ones. Coach Helmut Schoen was certain his squad had the talent to reach the final.

The West Germans bucked tradition, and allowed Brazil to play the first game of the tournament against Yugoslavia. The decision was hardly a magnanimous one. West Ger-

many noted that the host country often opened the World Cup nervously, and wanted to avoid an early stumble. As if on cue, the Brazilians had their troubles with the Yugos. In a driving rain storm, the defending champs sloshed their way to a scoreless tie. West Germany also struggled in its opener, grinding out a 1-0 win over Chile while their fans booed and jeered their lifeless play. Italy had its problems, too. The Haitian team drew first blood in their opener, and it took a great game by Zoff to turn things around and produce a 3-1 win. The Poles had no such troubles. They disposed of Argentina with relative ease.

As the first round progressed, it became clear which teams were likely to contend for the title. West Germany was the class of Group 1, despite losing 1-0 to its Communist neighbor in East Germany. Yugoslavia finished ahead of Brazil in Group 2, thanks to a 9-0 drubbing of Zaire. In Group 3, Holland prevailed, while the Poles moved out of Group 4.

Thanks to a format change, the eight teams advancing from the opening round were regrouped into two new groups for a second round of matches. The winner of each group would then meet in the final. The reason for this shift in policy was—what else?—money. The new format would produce a few more games.

Holland, Argentina, Brazil, and East Germany made up Group A. The Dutch dominated the Argentinians and East Germans in their first two games, blanking both opponents. Brazil beat the same two squads, setting up a match against Holland to decide who would play in the final. Neither team scored in the first half, though Brazil did a fair amount of damage with its rough and sometimes dirty tactics. The Dutch responded by throwing their weight around in the second half, giving the Brazilians a small dose of their own medicine. With the defense softened up, Cruyff footed a pass to Neeskens, who found the net for a, 1-0, lead. Minutes later Cruyff scored to put the game out of reach.

In Group B, West Germany and Poland rushed toward a similar showdown. Both teams beat Yugoslavia and Sweden, then squared off to see who would get a crack at the Dutch. Game day brought a terrific downpour and great puddles, which were "squeegeed" off the field by firemen. Still, the playing surface was a sloppy mess. This favored the disciplined Germans, while slowing down Poland's fastest players, Lato and Gadocha. When Maier robbed Poland with several great saves in the first half,

Johan Cruyff triggers the Dutch attack against Sweden during World Cup 74.

West Germany began to control the match. The second half opened with a penalty kick for the Germans, but Polish goal-keeper Jan Tomaszewski made the stop to preserve the scoreless deadlock. Finally, Muller broke the ice with a goal, and West Germany advanced, 1-0.

Prior to the championship match, fans shifted anxiously in their seats during the endless pomp and ceremony. A choir of 1,5000 singers performed "Tulips from Amsterdam," followed by a peppy version of "Ode to Joy." Dignitaries from around the globe, including (German-born) U.S. Secretary of State Henry Kissinger, slowly took their seats. Next came each country's national anthem. Then there was another delay, after it was discovered that the corner flags had not yet been hammered into the ground.

When the game finally started, it seemed that West Germany still wasn't ready. Holland zipped down the field with a series of quick passes. When Cruyff penetrated into the penalty area, the Germans had no choice but to foul him, giving the Dutch the first penalty kick ever in a World Cup final. Neeskens calmly fired a shot past Maier for the fastest goal in tournament history. Though overjoyed, Dutch fans had to wonder: was this goal a curse? In six previous finals, the team on the board first went on to lose. It was also well known that West Germany played best when backed into a corner.

Coach Michels, taking a page from his opponent's book, collapsed into a defensive shell, intent on nursing its lead. This proved to be a mistake, for it took Holland out of its game and allowed West Germany to probe for scoring opportunities without too much worry about a counter-attack. Midway through the first half, a questionable foul was whistled against the Dutch and a

Franz Beckenbauer battles for possession with Johan Neeskens. Both players blended refined skills with steely toughness.

brilliant, back-and-forth soccer. Cruyff and Beckenbauer, in the spotlight throughout, were fantastic. Holland took the initiative in the opening minutes, pounding the ball into the German defense again and again, but came up empty thanks to the cool play of Beckenbauer and Maier. As the game wore on, Cruyff chose to lay back and wait for opportunities to develop, instead of developing opportunities himself. The Germans smartly froze him out, and held on to win, 2-1.

Beckenbauer led the celebration when the final whistle blew, clutching the new trophy and thrusting it toward the adoring crowd. In the Dutch locker room, a distraught Cruyff lamented, "Germany didn't win. We lost it." That may well have been the case. But no one could dispute that the ultimate winner was World Cup 74 itself—on the field, at the turnstiles, and in the accounting ledgers.

penalty kick was awarded. Paul Breitner converted, and the game was tied.

The rest of the first half was exciting. At one point Berti Vogts raced towards the Dutch goal and fired a wicked blast, but keeper Jan Jongbloed batted it away. Moments later, Beckenbauer was foiled when his free kick was stopped by Jongbloed. The Dutch claimed the next scoring opportunity, as Cruyff fed Rep with a beautiful pass. Maier cut down the angle and made a masterful save. As time was running out in the first half, Muller corralled a ball in the Dutch penalty area and blasted a perfect shot past Jongbloed to give his team a 2-1 edge.

The second half action was a continuation of the first half, as the two teams played

West German goalkeeper Sepp Maier poses for photographers with the Jules Rimet Trophy after defeating Holland.

POWER PLAYER:
FRANZ BECKENBAUER—GERMANY

No soccer figure in recent times has left a greater imprint on the World Cup than Franz Beckenbauer. In 1966, he led his West German team all the way to the final, where they lost on a controversial goal. In 1970 he sparked a stirring comeback against England with a magnificent goal in the quarterfinals. In 1974, Beckenbauer led his nation to the championship and was hailed as the most valuable player in the world.

After his playing days, he succeeded Jupp Derwall as coach of the national team. This was considered a huge gamble—the German system promoted from within, and Beckenbauer was an outsider with no coaching experience on any level. The move paid off when he led the team to the World Cup final in 1986 and won it all in 1990 to become the first to accomplish this feat as both a player and manager.

His fans were hardly surprised. The qualities that made Beckenbauer a great player—and pioneer of the attacking "sweeper" position—served him equally well as coach. He could look at any part of the field during any stage of a game, know instinctively what scenarios were likely to develop, and then move to either support or prevent them. To this day, no one has read the field as well as "Kaiser Franz."

Franz Beckenbauer and coach Helmut Schoen rejoice in victory after their 2-1 win over Holland in the 1974 World Cup final.

GREAT PLAYER:
GERD MULLER—WEST GERMANY

"One-dimensional" soccer players rarely make it to the World Cup. It is generally accepted, in fact, that doing only one thing, even if you do it well, won't earn one a spot on a national team. Gerd Muller was the exception to this rule. He could not run, dribble, pass, or defend. He could not create his own shot, and he had no style whatsoever. What Muller could do was score. If there was a loose ball within 20 yards of the goal, Muller was on it with his leg cocked for a hard, accurate shot. It was amazing. He seemed to know when and where the ball would squirt loose, and he moved to that spot while everyone else was moving somewhere else. His 68 goals

Gerd Muller (l) and Paul Bretiner (r) display the look of champions after helping West Germany win World Cup 74.

in 62 international matches—and record 365 goals in German Bundesliga play—earned him the nickname, "Der Bomber." Muller's most famous "bomb" was the one that blew open the 1974 World Cup final.

Winner: West Germany
Runner-up: Holland
Best Player: Franz Beckenbauer

1978
Argentina

The sideswiping of politics and sports brought about by the World Cup every four years was especially evident in 1978. When FIFA selected Argentina to be the host country earlier in the decade, the iron-fisted Peronistas were in control in Buenos Aires. The government spent millions in preparation for World Cup 78, financing the construction of three brand new stadiums, a massive road-paving program, and the introduction of color television.

In 1976, the Montoneros guerrilla movement seized power in Argentina, causing many in the international soccer community to request a change of venue for the tournament. FIFA president Joao Havelange could not be swayed. He preferred to stick with Argentina and work with the Montoneros, who convinced him that staging the

The 1978 World Cup host team Argentina. Many in the soccer community pushed to have the tournament played elsewhere because of civil unrest.

World Cup was a great way to unite the Argentinian people.

When the matches began, Holland was the overwhelming favorite. Its program of Total Soccer had evolved since World Cup 74, and they now were expected to literally "run circles" around their opponents. Or were they? The team's new coach, Ernst Happel, had been nudging his players more toward the growing European trends of speed and power, and away from the thinking man's game that had so impressed fans. The embodiment of this new focus was Johan Neeskens, the tireless midfielder who was now rated among the very best in the world. Noticeable by his absence was Johan Cruyff, who chose not to compete.

Looking to knock off the Dutch were Scotland and its boastful coach, Ally MacLeod, as well as West Germany, which

was without superstar Franz Beckenbauer for the first time since World Cup 66. Brazil, always a threat to win it all, was still adjusting to its new coach, Claudio Coutinho. His demanding methods included a lot of extra fitness training and complex strategies. Brazilian fans had a feeling that this would stifle the instinctive brilliance of players like Zico and Rivelino.

Argentina was also in the mix, as the World Cup host almost always is. However, the country's top players were not. Coach Cesar Luis Menotti decided against using stars who played professionally in foreign leagues and instead picked a team of "All-Stars" from Argentina's pro league and trained them together for the tournament. This created a couple of problems. First, some of the most famous Argentinian players would not be playing for their country. Second, the national clubs all had to agree to release their best players so Menotti could mold them into a cohesive unit. He eventually twisted enough arms to get the squad he wanted. It was led by Daniel Bertoni, Osvaldo Ardiles, and captain Daniel Passarella—all of whom were at their best with the ball at their feet. Mario Kempes, playing in Spain for the Valencia club, was the only foreign-based player recalled.

In the opening round, Menotti looked more like an idiot than a genius. The home team won a sloppy game with Hungary, then squeaked through a close match with France on a late goal by Leopoldo Luque. Argentina was soundly beaten by Italy in its next game, but had enough points to advance.

Meanwhile, Holland advanced, but not

Johan Cruyff, who chose not to compete in 1978. Holland reached the final anyway.

without an eyebrow-raising loss to the Scots. The win was not enough to keep Scotland afloat, however, as they had earlier lost to Peru and were sent packing. The West Germans also encountered problems in their group. A dreary, scoreless tie with Poland had to be one of the worst matches in tournament history. And although the Germans rebounded to destroy Mexico, they had to settle for a surprising draw with Tunisia. The Tunisia game turned out to be an important one. There had been a growing movement to expand the World Cup field so that more African nations might qualify. Tunisia's performance against West Germany would be a crucial piece of ammunition for those in favor of expansion.

Brazil was the fourth favorite that struggled to advance. As many feared, the team had yet to find its rhythm. A game-winning goal by Zico was waved off when time expired against Sweden, and Brazil had to settle for a tie. The team tied its next game, against Spain, and barely got past Austria, 1-0. Though relieved to still be in the hunt, Brazil's fans had seen enough; a stuffed dummy of Coach Coutinho was set ablaze outside the stadium.

With no clear-cut "hot" team, World Cup 78 was declared wide open. That is when the Dutch stepped up and started playing the kind of soccer everyone expected. They shellacked Austria 5-1, then engaged in an epic battle with West Germany. The two 1974 finalists went at each other like two prizefighters in this match. The Germans struck first, scoring an early goal. But Holland knotted the score. Another German goal was answered by Rene Van de Kerkhof, who scored with eight minutes remaining for a, 2-2, tie. Holland then beat Italy 2-1, recovering nicely from a gaffe by Erny Brandts, who scored on his own keeper. The young fullback atoned for his miscue by drilling home the tying goal. Then Arie Haan put Holland in front for good a few minutes later, and the Dutch were on their way back to the final.

On the other side of the draw, both Brazil and Argentina won once before battling each other to a scoreless tie. This meant the second finalist would likely be determined by goal differential. Brazil played first, and defeated Poland soundly, 3-1. Because Brazil had outscored Argentina to that point, Argentina needed to beat Peru by at least four goals to make it to the final.

What happened next was called the "Game of Shame." Peru's goal-keeper, who was born in Argentina, did not want to go down in history as the most hated man in his country of origin. His teammates also had it in mind to let heavily favored Argentina run up the score. Anticipating this turn of events, wealthy Brazilian fans camped out in the hotel where the Peruvian players were staying, and offered them suitcases of money and large tracts of land in Brazil in exchange for giving their best effort. Although it is against the rules to bribe a player to give less than his best effort, there is nothing that specifically forbids a "bonus" aimed at making someone simply play to the best of their abilities.

Except maybe common sense. At this level of pro soccer, if a player's heart isn't in the game, no amount of money will make him give his all. And apparently that is what happened. The Brazilian fans watched in horror as Argentina pumped in goal after goal after goal against Peru. The 6-0 final score vaulted the home team into the final, and just to rub it in, their fans chanted "Llora Brasil, llora!" (Weep Brazil, Weep) throughout the game.

Although many still questioned Menotti's "fulbito" (little football) approach, he and his players were no longer under such intense scrutiny by their own fans, who had fallen passionately in love with the team. Their deep, emotional outpouring of affection filled the players with pride and confidence, and this made them an extremely dangerous club. No one was more aware of this than the Dutch, who had run into a similar situation four years earlier.

The mood in Argentina became increasingly electric as the final approached. Throughout the tournament, the hometown fans had rooted for their team with unabashed enthusiasm. Whenever Argentina took the field, a shower of streamers and confetti known as "papelitos" rained down on the playing surface. Argentinian flags waved everywhere.

Both teams were highly confident. As they had throughout the World Cup, Menotti's men planned to attack with quickness and intelligence. For their part, the Dutch were playing a particularly breathtaking brand of soccer, and seemed to be coming together at just the right time.

Menotti employed a bit of gamesmanship when he held his players under the stands for an extra 10 minutes, while the Dutch players milled about on the field, looking anxious and irritated. Argentina then emerged to thunderous cheering. Before the kickoff, the coach demanded that referees inspect an arm cast being worn by Van de Kerkhof. Though he had used the protective device for the entire tournament, the Argentinians forced him to follow the letter of the rules and switch to a bandage.

POWER PLAYER:
MARIO KEMPES—ARGENTINA

Cesar Luis Menotti stirred up a hornets' nest of controversy in 1978 when he decided to use local players to build Argentina's World Cup squad. There were at least a dozen Argentinian stars playing abroad at the time, and many fans thought their international experience would be crucial in the tournament. But Menotti held firm on his decision—with one exception. Mario Kempes, the relentless 25-year-old international striker, was a must-have player.

Kempes hit defenses like a hammer comes down on an anvil. He was big and fast and had legs like tree trunks. In World Cup 78 he led all players in goals, with his last two coming against Holland in the final. Great things were predicted for Kempes after the tournament, but he never again approached the level of dominance he displayed before his home fans that summer.

Dashing Mario Kempes surveys the Belgian defense. He was voted the tournament's top player in 1978.

Holland retaliated once the match began, as Jan Poortvliet tripped Bertoni from behind, then Arie Haan unloaded on Ardiles. Both fouls were highly uncharacteristic of the normally disciplined Dutch. The game, though penalty-ridden, quickly developed into an offensive flurry, with both teams attacking whenever an opportunity presented itself. The frenzied pace put a premium on goal-keeping, and both netminders were up to the task. Argentina's Ubaldo Fillol made a brilliant save on a shot by Johnny Rep. Holland's Jan Jongbloed matched him with two great plays against Passarella. Kempes finally solved the Dutch goal-keeper eight minutes before halftime, taking a pass from Luque and skirting the ball along the ground into the net. Moments later Robby Rensenbrink had a chance to tie it for Holland, but Fillol came up with a big save.

The Dutch opened the second half by increasing the pressure on Argentina's defense. Coach Happel substituted Dirk Nanninga for Rep to get fresh legs in the game, and the move would pay huge dividends. As the match progressed and Argentina clung to its precious lead, the crowd roared louder and louder. Holland, meanwhile, worked

Argentine captain Daniel Passarella grips the Jules Rimet Trophy after defeating Holland in the 1978 final.

even harder to tie the score. In the 81st minute Nanninga leapt high in the air and headed a ball past a sprawling Fillol to tie the score at 1-1. The goal immediately silenced the crowd, which now feared the momentum on the field had shifted.

Menotti's crew responded like champions. When the match moved into overtime, the Argentinians seized control. Kempes struck first, following up his own shot with another that he sent by Jongbloed. Minutes later he helped seal victory by setting up Bertoni for a goal that made the final score 3-1.

When time finally ran out, fans throughout Buenos Aires erupted in a rapturous celebration. Argentina had won its first World Cup. The streets were filled with singing, dancing, and laughing, as

parties continued wild abandon for days. The tournament did indeed bring joy back to the people of Argentina, and the Montoneros, led by President Jorge Videla, joined the rest of the country in hailing Menotti as a genius.

> **Winner: Argentina**
> **Runner-up: Holland**
> **Best Player: Mario Kempes**

1982
Spain

The world had become a much more complicated place since World Cup 78. Argentina and England were at war over the Falkland Islands, the Soviet Union had invaded Afghanistan, and Iran had been transformed into a terrorist state by Muslim fundamentalists. President Ronald Reagan and Pope John Paul II had been targeted by assassins, and survived. Egyptian leader Anwar Sadat had not been so lucky. Against this backdrop of unrest and violence, World Cup 82 began.

The tournament featured a couple of important changes. First, the field had grown from 16 entrants to 24. And games played in the elimination rounds would now be decided by a shootout from the penalty stripe after a scoreless overtime, with each side getting five kicks.

Worldwide television viewership would provide the greatest audience yet for a World Cup. Spain, now fully awakened after shaking off one of the world's last old-time fascist regimes, meant to make the tournament a true spectacle. Organizers lavished attention and spent countless millions on every last detail, including the official mascot, "Naranjito," a gigantic walking orange. The opening ceremonies were breathtaking.

The competition featured several superb teams. Despite losing its emerging star, Bernd Schuster, to a knee injury, West Germany still had Karl-Heinz Rummenigge, Paul Breitner, and Hans-Peter Briegel. New coach Jupp Derwall also possessed a secret weapon: his team trained with an energy drink called MS-61, which was supposed to increase strength and stamina. France also had a fearsome club. Built around the immensely gifted Michel Platini, the French were known as "the "Brazilians of Europe" for their artistic style of play. Among the South American teams, Brazil—under the steady hand of coach Tele Santana—came with the most impressive roster of international stars, including Zico, Junior, Socrates, and Toninho Cerezo.

Another team worth watching was Italy. Forty-year-old goal-keeper Dino Zoff, the team captain, was smart and experienced. In front of him Gaetano Scirea was the best sweeper in the world, while Giancarlo Antognoni, Fulvio Collovati, and Antonio Cabrini anchored a suffocating defense. The only thing the Italians seemed to lack was a bona fide goal scorer, so coach Enzo Bearzot took a chance. Two years earlier Paolo Rossi had been suspended for his role in a game-fixing scandal, and had not played competitively since. Bearzot named Rossi to the team, then put him in the starting lineup. Could this once brilliant scorer regain his form?

Early on it appeared that Bearzot had made a mistake. Positioned in Group 1 with Poland, Cameroon, and Peru, Italy managed three ties, and netted a total of only two goals. With the press hounding them

for an explanation, the Italians decided they would boycott all reporters. Anytime they were asked a question, they would say, "Talk to the captain." The captain, Zoff, was notorious for being the toughest interview in the sport.

West Germany also experienced early struggles. In its first game, the team was upset by Algeria, 2-1. They rebounded with a 4-1 pasting of Chile. That set up a match against Austria, its European neighbor. If Germany won the game by a score of 1-0, then both countries would move on to elimination play, and the plucky Algerians would be out of the picture. After the Germans scored, neither team made a serious

Dino Zoff of Italy. The 40-year-old's goalkeeping helped his team win the World Cup in 1982.

attempt to rush the net, and the final count was indeed 1-0. It was a dirty way to play, and the Algerians protested, but FIFA ignored their pleas.

France survived its group, but not without incident. Ahead 3-0 against Kuwait, the French appeared to score a fourth goal. The Kuwaitis claimed that they had stopped playing defense because their opponents had been whistled offsides. At first, officials upheld the goal ruling. But the wealthy, powerful Sheik Fahed—who also happened to be head of Kuwait's soccer federation—stormed onto the field to express his displeasure. A few minutes later the call was reversed and the goal disallowed. It was the first of many questionable decisions by the referees during the tournament.

As expected, Brazil was rolling, too. In successive victories over the USSR, Scotland, and New Zealand, Santana's club played near-perfect soccer. The buzz in the stands was that the Brazilians were better than ever. They would have to be, for in the next round they were placed in Group C with Argentina and Italy. The Argentinians had advanced despite the harsh treatment of their 21-year-old star Diego Maradona. He was pushed, shoved, grabbed, and kicked repeatedly in the first round, but the referees turned a blind eye to the obvious fouls. Naturally, Brazil and Italy employed the same tactics, and both wound up defeating Argentina.

This set up a match between Brazil and Italy to determine who would reach the semifinals. Brazil could advance with a draw, while the Italians needed a victory. Coach Bearzot had his full compliment of players, thanks to the blind eye of the referees, who should have given Claudio Gentile a red card for his brutal treatment of Maradona in the Argentina game. With Gentile available to intimidate Zico, the Italians had a decent chance. To win, however, they would need a big game from Rossi, who still had not found the net.

The veteran finally broke the ice in the first half against Brazil, giving his team a 1-0 lead. The crafty Zico broke loose, however, and knotted the score. But Rossi came right back and scored again for Italy to make it 2-1. Brazil continued to attack Italy's vaunted defense until Falcao drilled a shot that re-tied the game. With just 20 minutes, left, all Brazil had to do was tighten up on defense and preserve the tie. But that was not the team's nature. They wanted a win in the worst way, and they went for the jugular. This proved to be the mistake of the tournament, as Brazil left its defense too spread out and Italy counter-attacked. Once again it was Rossi finishing, and Brazil found itself out of the World Cup with a 3-2 defeat.

Rossi continued his heroics in the semifinals, scoring both goals in a 2-0 victory over Poland to secure a spot in the finals. There Italy would face West Germany, which had walked a very fine line indeed. After narrowly escaping their second-round grouping (with England and Spain), the West Germans appeared to have lost 3-1 to France in the semis. But during the extra time tacked on by the referees, both Rummenigge and Klaus Fischer scored on controversial plays to tie the game, which eventually led to a shootout. From there, keeper Toni Schumacher took over and made a couple of big saves, and West Germany advanced. To this day, French fans wonder why Schumacher was even on the field at this point. Earlier in the game, he had knocked Patrick Battiston out cold with a kick to the head, but the referees refused to penalize him. In a tournament full of lousy officiating, this one was the worst example.

Under normal circumstances, international soccer fans would have split their allegiances between Italy and West Germany. But most felt the Germans had gained the final unfairly, and thus rooted for Italy. A headline in an English newspaper that blared "These Cheats Must Not Win It" was typical of the resentment harbored around the globe.

Of the two clubs, Italy was the better rested. Their only injury was to Antognoni, who was on the bench with a sore foot. The West Germans had expended a tremendous amount of energy against France, and Rummenigge was particularly worn down. For a time, it appeared he would not even be able to start the game.

The day began badly for Italy, when Francesco Graziani dislocated his shoulder on a hard tackle by Wolfgang Dremmler. Things looked up briefly when Cabrini was fouled in the penalty box, but he muffed his kick, sending it high over the bar. When the first half ended there was no score, and neither team had gained any real advantage.

In the second half, Italy decided to put its fresher legs to work. The team pressed the attack against West Germany and finally it began to pay off. Once again it was Rossi who broke the ice, scoring his sixth consecutive goal for the Italians. Scirea made the next big play, delivering a perfect pass to Marco Tardelli, who gave his team a 2-0 lead. Alessandro Altobelli, substituting for Graziani, capped Italy's offensive outburst 11 minutes later with a third goal. Breitner netted one for the Germans, but it was too little, too late.

There was no question that Italy had earned the championship, and that Rossi had played his way back into the good graces of soccer fans. There was also complete agreement on the quality of the refereeing: it was

Marco Tardelli leads the charge as Italy celebrates its second goal of the 1982 final. The Italians stunned West Germany, 3-1.

Argentine goalkeeper Nery Pumpido celebrates his team's World Cup victory.

POWER PLAYER: PAOLO ROSSI—ITALY

No World Cup hero took a more twisted path to international superstardom than Italy's Paolo Rossi. Signed as a schoolboy by the powerhouse Juventus club in the early 1970s, he developed knee trouble and was released while still a teenager. Rossi recovered sufficiently to become a star for the Como and Lanerossi Vicenza clubs, displaying a knack for scoring big goals. A few years later, realizing their mistake, Juventus tried to buy him back, but was outbid by another club, which paid 3.5 million pounds for his services—a world record that stood for four years.

After starring for Italy at World Cup 78, Rossi became embroiled in a match-fixing scandal. Although never convicted of a crime, he was banned from soccer for two years. Rossi came back to finish the last two weeks of the season for Juventus in 1982 before being assigned to the national team. Playing his way into shape as the World Cup progressed, this magical scorer did more than anyone expected, lifting the "Azzuri" to a totally unexpected championship. Despite having played a mere three games outside of the World Cup in 1982, he was nonetheless voted European Footballer of the Year.

Three seasons later, at the age of 29, Rossi was forced to quit. His old injuries had finally caught up with him and he could play no more.

inexcusably bad. In a world where no one could seem to agree on anything, it was nice to see that soccer fans were on the same page when it came to their sport.

> **Winner: Italy**
> **Runner-up: West Germany**
> **Best Player: Paolo Rossi**

1986
Mexico

Soccer can affect people in many ways. It can inspire them. It can anger them. It can leave them in awe. The 1986 World Cup did all these things, and more. In a wildly entertaining tournament, fans were treated to the full spectrum of thrills and chills. The player who authored many of these moments was Argentina's incomparable Diego Maradona, who used World Cup 86 as a launchpad to immortality.

That Mexico was able to host one match, much less the entire World Cup, was a miracle in itself. In September of 1985, 10 months before the tournament was set to start, a powerful earthquake ripped through Mexico City, killing thousands and creating a not-so-small army of homeless that had to be sheltered and fed. The strain on Mexican society was profound, but the people persevered, buoyed by the thought that in less than a year the whole world would be watching them.

Ironically, Mexico hadn't been the initial choice to stage the World Cup. FIFA had awarded the honor to Colombia. But with the country's economy struggling and its security compromised by powerful drug lords, an unprecedented change was made. Mexico—the World Cup's first two-time host—was selected in part because of a lucrative agreement reached between its leading private television company and FIFA.

Despite the built-in advantage of having the home fans behind them, Mexico's players did not figure to be much of a threat. They were clearly outclassed by the three tournament favorites: Argentina, Brazil, and France. This trio was given the edge over talented squads from England and West Germany, which played with a more wide-open, attacking style. It was believed that the heat of the Mexican sun would make this approach difficult to sustain. This was a definite factor, for once again many of the games involving European teams had been scheduled for the afternoon, so games could be aired across the Atlantic in primetime. As it had in 1970, this seemed to favor the more conservative clubs.

Argentina boasted the best player in the tournament in Maradona. He was an artist with the ball who could dribble, pass, and shoot as well as anyone in the world. He also had an intangible quality for coming up big in important games. Maradona's World Cup legacy, however, was still a work in progress. To this point his most memorable moment on the big stage was being ejected for kicking a Brazilian opponent, in Spain, during World Cup 82. Whatever Maradona hoped to accomplish this time around, he would have to do it on a bum knee. It was more of a nagging injury than a serious one, but no one could be sure how it would affect his play.

The top European player at World Cup 86 was Michel Platini of France. At 31, he knew this might be his final appearance. Karl-Heinz Rummenigge of West Germany was in the same boat. Also in his 30s, he still felt the sting of losing to Italy in the final four years earlier. The captain of that squad, Franz Beckenbauer, was now West Germany's coach. The ascending player on the national team was Lothar Matthaus.

The Group A draw included Argentina and Italy, which naturally made it the most-watched. The defending champs struggled in the hot, humid atmosphere, with one win and two ties. Argentina fared much better, defeating South Korea and Bulgaria, and playing Italy to a stand-off. Much to the relief of Carlos Bilardo, the new Argentinian coach, Maradona showed no signs of poor health. This was crucial, because Bilardo preferred to play his other men cautiously. If Maradona was less than 100 percent, he would have had to shift strategies in order to get more scoring opportunities.

Meanwhile, Beckenbauer, in an attempt to conserve energy, modified West Germany's attacking style and found a measure of success. The Germans made their way to the Round of 16 with a win over Scotland and a draw with Uruguay. France advanced, too, but Platini seemed to be searching for his rhythm, which worried French fans. The heat was definitely a factor. No one knew this better than England, which had fielded its most exciting team in 20 years. Superstars Gary Lineker and Peter Beardsley were unable to jump-start the offense, and the Brits—whose fans harbored high hopes of winning it all—barely escaped Group F. On balance, however, opening-round play was quite good.

The same could not be said for the opening-round television coverage. Mexico's Televisa network, charged with beaming the action around the world, performed like the gang that couldn't shoot straight. Some countries got a great picture but no sound. Others got great sound but no picture. Many who got picture and sound were stunned to hear the action described in a strange language. Millions of Brazilian fans, for instance, had to choose between turning off the sound or listening to their games in Italian. Colombian fans had to endure games announced in Portuguese. Finally, FIFA stepped in and threatened to ruin Televisa with a multibillion dollar lawsuit. All the problems were magically corrected.

The first tense moment of the tournament occurred when West Germany found itself in a struggle with a surprisingly tough team from Morocco. The game was scoreless late in the second half, when Matthaus lined up a free kick. As he approached the ball he noticed the Moroccan defense had miscalculated and left an opening right through to the goal. He calmly blasted a shot into the back of the net and West Germany made it to the quarterfinals. Another shocker was Uruguay's fine play against Argentina. Although Maradona performed magnificently, the boys from Montevideo made great plays all game long. The Argentinians were lucky to escape with a 1-0 win. France and England had an easier time of it. Platini finally scored for "Les Bleus," while the English stars disposed of Paraguay with ease.

In the quarterfinals, the West Germans took on an inspired Mexican team, which was without its best playmaker, Tomas Boy. His absence was felt all day long, as neither club mounted much of an offensive attack. When the game went to penalty kicks, West Germany won easily. France overcame Brazil in a classic duel also decided by penalty kicks. The Brazilians moved ahead early, but Platini knotted the score at 1-1 and that's where it stayed right through extra time. During the penalty kicks, France was awarded a controversial goal on a shot that caromed off the post, hit Brazil's goalkeeper in the back, and bounced into the net. It turned out to be the decisive tally and France advanced to the semis.

The most compelling match was between Argentina and England. It was the first meeting between the countries since they had gone to war in the Falklands. Both teams had large, boisterous throngs in attendance. Soldiers and police—guns and clubs at the ready—were dispatched throughout the stadium to keep the peace. The battle on the field was just as tense. In the second half of a scoreless match, Steve Hodge attempted to lift a pass back to keeper Peter Shilton. Maradona made a mad dash for the goal and leapt into the air as Shilton reached for the ball. The two collided and the ball rolled into the net.

It was not immediately clear what had happened. The referee signaled that Maradona had scored. Instant replay revealed that Maradona had actually punched the ball with his hand and masterfully concealed it from the officials. After much discussion (replays were not available to the refs) the goal was allowed.

Minutes later Maradona was at it again, only this time he scored on a clean play.

Racing the length of the field, he weaved his way through five defenders with an eye-popping series of spins, twists, and fakes. When Shilton came out of the goal to stop him, he maneuvered around him, too. The goal, considered among the greatest individual accomplishments in World Cup history, clinched a 2-1 victory.

In the semifinals, West Germany squared off against France, and controlled the match—start to finish. Andy Brehme scored early for the West Germans, who nursed their 1-0 lead into intermission. France tried valiantly to mount a counter-attack, but Toni Schumacher stood tall in goal and Platini was all but worn out. When Rudi Voller added a final tally late in the match, the West Germans returned to the final for the second tournament in a row.

In the other semifinal contest, Maradona continued his brilliance against Belgium. As if he needed extra motivation, the Argentinian remembered the rough treatment he had received at the hands of the Belgians in his 1982 World Cup debut. Maradona scored twice in the second half, with both goals coming on extraordinary individual efforts. The overmatched Belgians had no response, and Argentina joined West Germany in the final.

For West Germany to win a third World Cup, Beckenbauer had to devise a way to stop Maradona. He decided that Matthaus and Karl-Heinz Foerster would share this responsibility. Bilardo, meanwhile, continued his strategy of using a core of excellent all-around midfielders to control the action, while letting Maradona penetrate and create havoc. From the opening kickoff, it was clear that West Germany was devoting too much attention to Maradona. Bilardo saw this and sent his other players rushing toward the net, which resulted in easy goals by Jose Luis Brown and Jorge Valdano. West Germany finally began to show signs of life in the second half after a bad offsides call ruined an Argentinian scoring chance. Rummenigge converted a corner kick by Brehme to cut the score to 2-1, then Voller scored on a near-identical play to produce a 2-2 deadlock.

Superstar Diego Maradona prepares to launch an attack in an opening-round match against Bulgaria. His play dominated the headlines during World Cup 86.

POWER PLAYER:
DIEGO MARADONA—ARGENTINA

Although no one could match the brilliance of Pele on the World Cup stage, the player who came closest was Diego Maradona of Argentina. An awesome natural talent, he had the uncanny ability to create goals out of thin air. His passing skills, which are often overlooked, were exquisite, too.

Maradona had an ideal body to go with his immense ability. He was short and stocky, with a center of gravity so low to the ground that he could not be muscled off the ball when it was at his feet. Maradona was also fast in the open field, as England discovered in 1986. Everyone may remember his "hand of god" goal in that match, but fans often forget that he later scored the game-winner on a 70-yard run that ranks among one of the most brilliant goals in World Cup history.

Argentina didn't panic. With extra time looming, Maradona took the ball in his own end. As several West Germans sped towards him, he spotted Jorge Burruchaga by himself at midfield. Waiting until the last possible moment, Maradona casually flipped a pass ahead, and his teammate was off to the races. Burruchaga's goal, in the 84th minute, proved to be the winner, as Argentina claimed its second title in eight years.

Argentina's victory was met with varied reactions throughout the soccer world. English fans would never forget the controversial Maradona goal. West Germany licked its wounds, but immediately set about the task of gearing up for World Cup 90. Bilardo became a hero in his homeland. And Maradona became a soccer god. The real winners, however, were the Mexican people. The thrilling tournament helped them forget their troubles and re-energized the country as they continued on the long road to recovery.

> **Winner: Argentina**
> **Runner-up: West Germany**
> **Best Player: Diego Maradona**

1990
Italy

As World Cup 90 approached, anticipation in Italy rose to unprecedented levels. The Italians billed the event as the "People's World Cup," and promised to make it the best ever. There were some, however, who viewed the festivities with a cynical eye. The World Cup had been conceived as a global celebration of soccer. Now it appeared that money and marketing ruled the day. The Italians were selling every conceivable kind of sponsorship opportunity, with little regard for maintaining the "look" of the tournament. Those who criticized FIFA for allowing this "soiling" of soccer were equally horrified by what they saw on the field once the games began. Scoring dropped drastically, as dirty tactics and questionable calls dominated the action.

Anyone who had been watching soccer during the previous year could not have been surprised. Weird things had been happening on soccer fields all over the world. At the 1989 World Youth Championship, for instance, Mexico tried to stock its club with overaged players. When FIFA uncovered the scandal, Mexico's national team was banned from World Cup play. Perhaps the strangest incident occurred in a qualifying match between Chile and heavily favored Brazil. A spectator ignited a flare and hurled it toward the Chilean goal. Keeper Roberto Rojas fainted dead away when he saw this, and was carried from the field by his teammates. Chile's players, claiming they feared for their lives, refused to take the field and pushed for a forfeit. FIFA investigated the incident and discovered the entire thing had been carefully orchestrated by the Chilean team. Rojas was suspended for life and Chile was denied the victory.

The hands-down favorite to win the World Cup was Italy. A talented group playing in front of enthusiastic home crowds, the Italian team was coached by Azeglio Vicini and starred Paolo Maldini, Franco Baresi, and Roberto Baggio. The club's Achilles heel was the immense pressure and high expectations under which the players and their coach labored; nothing short of a championship would be acceptable, and to a man they knew it.

Guido Buchwald and Lothar Matthaus sandwich Diego Maradona in the 1990 final. Plays like this one enraged Argentine players and fans, who claimed the referees were favoring European squads.

Holland, led by wonderfully talented midfielder Ruud Gullit, stood poised to grab the title if Italy faltered. So too, did the 1986 finalists, Argentina and West Germany. The West Germans, coached again by Franz Beckenbauer, were a disciplined squad that had achieved a spectacular balance between defense and offense under his tutelage. Argentina, the defending champ, was beginning to show its age, particularly the once fabulous Diego Maradona, who had lost a step and gained a few pounds in four years. Although Argentina had historically experienced problems playing outside South America, coach Carlos Bilardo remained optimistic.

The ugliness began in Milan, in a Group B game between Argentina and Cameroon. It was a rough, penalty-filled match won by Cameroon, which became an instant fan favorite after veteran Roger Milla led his team to a 1-0 victory despite only having nine men on the field. Argentina's woes continued, as Maradona and company barely beat Russia and settled for a tie with the Romanians. The good news was that they managed to sneak into the Round of 16. The bad news was that goal-keeper Nery Pumpido was out with a broken leg. Bilardo had no choice but to turn to back-up Sergio Goycochea.

In Group D, West Germany was rolling right along. Lothar Matthaus tallied two goals in a 4-1 blowout of Yugoslavia, and starred again as his team drubbed the United Arab Emirates, 5-1. Assured of a spot in the Round of 16, the West Germans fought Colombia to a tie in its third group match. These games were cleanly played, but violence exploded outside the stadium after the Germans' second win. Their fans went on a rampage through the streets of Milan, getting into scuffles, damaging prop-

erty and causing nearly two dozen injuries. The Italians were expecting problems with fans, but not these fans. The authorities were far more concerned with England's famous soccer hooligans. In fact, FIFA had scheduled England's games on the island of Sardinia just so they could more easily control the troublemakers.

Throughout the early rounds, however, the attention of the Italian fans was riveted on their own team, which shutout Austria, the United States, and Czechoslovakia. Their surprise player was reserve Salvatore "Toto" Schillaci. Coach Vicini inserted him against Austria, and the smallish center forward promptly scored a goal. Before long Toto was the toast of Italy.

Brazil, which also reached the Round of 16, raised a lot of eyebrows with its new lineup. Employing a sweeper and reducing the number of forwards in its offense to two, the club meant to concentrate on its defense. This made no sense to a lot of observers, including Pele, who was widely quoted as saying this strategy would not work. He was proven correct in his country's match against Argentina, when Brazil failed to mount a sustained attack and fell, 1-0. The key play came courtesy of some Maradona magic. Dribbling in traffic, he lured no fewer than four defenders to his area before putting a perfect pass through to Claudio Caniggia, who was wide open. His goal ended Brazil's dream of regained glory and made Argentina a serious threat to reach the championship game.

That threat was met head-on by the Italian team, in a semifinal match played in laid-back Naples instead of bustling Rome. The crowd was small and quiet, which seemed to sap some of the team's energy. Still, Italy opened up a first-half lead on a lovely goal by Schillaci. Caniggia knotted the game for Argentina in the second half, and ended a 500-minute streak during which keeper Walter Zenga had blanked Italy's opponents. Italy fought hard to win, but Argentina fought back harder. In fact, Caniggia, Sergio Batista, and Ricardo Giusti each received red cards for their rough play, eliminating them from further appearances in the tournament. Neither team could find the net again, and the match was decided on kicks. Goycochea proved up to the task, outdueling the Italian shooters and sending Argentina to its second straight final.

Meanwhile, West Germany was doing its part to set up a finals rematch with the Argentinians. Against a surprisingly porous Dutch defense, Jurgen Klinsmann gave West Germany the lead in the first half and Andy Brehme added a second-half tally to seal the outcome. In the quarterfinals, the Germans dispatched Czechoslovakia 1-0 on a goal by Matthaus. That set up a match against England, which was settled by penalty kicks after neither team could break a 1-1 deadlock. When Stuart Pearce and Chris Waddle missed for England, West Germany advanced to its record sixth final.

In the days leading up to the championship game, disappointed Italians jeered the Argentine players when they encountered them in public, and hurled stones at the house in Naples where Maradona was known to be staying. When Argentina's national anthem was played, prior to the final, Italian fans whistled loudly.

Denied the services of three of his top players, Coach Bilardo knew his team's best chance was to slow the match to a crawl. Argentina fell back and made like a stonewall. Whenever a West German ventured too close to the goal, he was roughly treated. Pedro Monzon's aggressive play was so flagrant that he became the first player ever tossed out of a World Cup final. No one liked to see this kind of game, but Argentina's strategy was effective, as their opponents could not score.

As time ticked away, the referees—invisible for so much of this World Cup—took center stage. After ignoring an obvious foul committed by a West German player, official Edgar Codesal called a questionable foul on Argentina. The ruling awarded

Five West German players rise in unison to block a free kick. Argentina could not solve West Germany's defense in the 1990 final, and fell 1-0.

West German superstar Lothar Matthaus, one of the game's best players and most dynamic leaders.

Brehme a penalty kick, which he blasted past Goycochea. That was the only goal of the match. West Germany, which had lost in the two previous finals, finally claimed its third World Cup.

As expected, Argentina complained bitterly. Maradona contended that FIFA had "fixed" the match for West Germany. Though his accusations were baseless, his sentiments were shared by many. Fans from all countries felt dissatisfied with the way the 1990 World Cup was decided. The style of soccer had been brutish and boring, and the tournament's commercialism left a bad taste in people's mouths. With the purity of their sport compromised, the people who loved soccer wondered whether the "People's World Cup" would ever recover.

> **Winner: West Germany**
> **Runner-up: Argentina**
> **Best Player: Lothar Matthaus**

1994
United States

What if FIFA staged the World Cup, and no one showed up? That is what soccer purists from other countries feared as the United States prepared to host the tournament in 1994. Polls indicated that no more than a quarter of Americans even knew the World Cup was being contested on their soil, and even fewer said they were likely to watch it on TV, much less purchase tickets.

There were also accusations in the air that FIFA had succumbed to excessive greed by holding the tournament in the U.S. The organization had awarded the World Cup in part because America's business community had promised them huge profits. FIFA officials countered that their mission had always been to promote soccer and increase the game's popularity around the world. What better place to achieve these goals, the federation maintained, than in the most diverse and thriving country on the planet?

With the sport's most ardent followers ready to attack FIFA and the U.S. for delivering a substandard, highly commercialized product, the World Cup opened under more scrutiny than ever before. Much to their surprise, they got the very opposite of what they anticipated. Despite sweltering summer temperatures, the tournament offered a compelling level of soccer in venues that even the pickiest fans found more than accommodating. Cities across the country hosted early-round matches, with the final set for the Rose Bowl in Pasadena, California. Attendance was strong everywhere, and in every city the visiting teams were made to feel right at home.

The exciting level of play was partly the result of new rules passed to encourage teams to attack more aggressively on offense, and clean up their tactics on defense. FIFA now awarded three points instead of two for wins in the first round, relaxed its off-sides rule, and cracked down on tackling from behind—a dangerous technique that often sent the sport's stars hobbling to the sidelines. The stage was set for a summer of clean, exciting soccer. Although the U.S. team did not figure to advance very far, it was FIFA's sincerest hope that the quality of soccer would further fuel excitement for the sport on World Cup 94's home turf.

As the tournament opened, there was much discussion about three teams that were not in the draw. France and England, both eliminated in qualifying, had gone home. Zambia's promising national team, which was wiped out in a plane crash on their way to a match with Senegal, was tragically absent.

Most of the pre-Cup attention was lavished upon the tournament favorite, Brazil. This was a powerhouse club. As always, the Brazilians boasted a potent offense, this time led by super scorers Bebeto and Romario. But the defense was equally impressive, with goal-keeper Claudio Taffarel backing up a smart, talented back line. Coach Carlos Alberto Parreira had reason to be confident heading into the first round, but he had his eye on the other contenders, including Argentina, Colombia, Holland, and Germany, which had been reunited after the Berlin Wall came down.

In any other year, Italy would have been mentioned in the same breath as these great clubs. Yet the Italians, while strong on paper, seemed flawed on the field. They struggled just to qualify, and the odds-makers had them as longshots instead of favorites. This despite the presence of Roberto Bag-

gio, a magnificent all-around player, and the stingy defensive style favored by coach Arrigo Sacchi.

The tournament got off to a rousing start with the U.S. facing off against Switzerland in Detroit's Silverdome. In the first World Cup match ever contested indoors (though the stadium's artificial turf had been replaced with grass), America gained a tie, and set the tone for the drama that would follow.

Roberto Baggio flashes to his right in a 1994 World Cup match against Ireland. The Italian star scored game-winning goals against Spain and Bulgaria, but was injured and exhausted in the final against Argentina.

Brazil, the class of Group B, took its first two matches against Russia and Cameroon, before settling for a tie with the Swedes. This cinched first place in the group for the Brazilians, who moved on to the next round along with Sweden. As expected, Romario and Bebeto were the big stars. Also making headlines were Oleg Salenko and Roger Milla. In Russia's 6-1 trouncing of Cameroon, Salenko established a World Cup mark with five goals. For the losers, the 42-year-old Milla notched the only goal, making him the oldest player ever to "tickle the twine" in a World Cup match.

In the other groups, Argentina, behind an aging, overweight Diego Maradona, looked good early, but soon faded and barely managed to advance. As expected, Germany and Holland also moved on to the Round of 16. Italy, meanwhile, was lucky to wiggle its way out of Group E. The team fell 1-0 to Ireland, then lost its goal-keeper to a red card 20 minutes into the next match, against Norway. The Italians somehow rallied, overcoming the Norwegians by a score of 1-0. Italy then tied Mexico 1-1, meaning they could only advance into the Round of 16 as a Wild Card, which depended on how Cameroon did. Fortunately, the Italians got the break they were hoping for when Salenko produced his record-setting outburst against the Africans.

The biggest story of the first round came when the U.S. unexpectedly pushed its way into the Round of 16. It was widely acknowledged that Team USA was in the draw because they were the host country. However, a stunning upset of Colombia—in front of a packed house at the Rose Bowl—lifted the U.S. out of Group A and made headlines the world over. The victory came thanks to a bizarre mix-up in the first half. The Colom-

bians, playing without their usual aplomb, found themselves in a tense battle with the pumped-up Americans, led by Alexi Lalas, Tony Meola, and Cobi Jones. Defender Andres Escobar inadvertently deflected a pass into his own goal, and it proved the difference in a 2-1 victory. Upon his return to Colombia, Escobar was gunned down by gangsters, who had reportedly lost millions because of his mistake.

U.S. fans, who had already been buying tickets in surprisingly large numbers, gained a new enthusiasm for their players and for World Cup soccer in general. When Team USA next faced Brazil, television viewership was sky-high. The millions who watched the match received a real education. The talent gap between the U.S. and a world-class club like Brazil was immense. Not even the seemingly close 1-0 score could hide this fact, as the Brazilians often appeared to be toying with the Americans, whose strategy was to prevent all scoring opportunities and hope for a miracle goal. They never even got close. They did get under the skin of at least one opponent, the star defender Leonardo, who was given a red card for elbowing.

The Brazilians next faced Holland in the quarterfinals. The Dutch had watched how the U.S. team kept the score down, and decided to imitate this strategy. They, too, hoped to frustrate Brazil, and capitalize on a mistake. But after a scoreless first half, Romario and Bebeto each broke through, scoring past goal-keeper Ed De Goey. Then Holland opened things up a bit and answered with two goals of its own to knot the score. With less than 10 minutes to go, the game was up for grabs. That is when the unlikeliest hero stepped forward and scored the winning goal for Brazil. Branco, a fullback playing only because of the suspension to Leonardo, came out of nowhere and squeezed off a great shot to deliver a 3-2 victory. In Brazil's semifinal match against Sweden, Romario made the difference, scoring the only goal late in the second half of a tight defensive battle.

Coming like a freight train on the other side of the draw were the surprising Italians, who continued to live on the edge. Against Spain in the Round of 16, Italy took the lead, 1-0, in the first half on a goal by Dino Baggio, Roberto's brother. But the Spaniards fought back to tie the score in the second half. They nearly went ahead minutes later, but Pagliuca made a stupendous leg save against Julio Salinas. This set the stage for Roberto Baggio, who angled a shot past the Spanish goal-keeper for a 2-1 lead. Spain mounted one last flurry, and appeared to have a golden opportunity to even the score when Italian defender Mauro Tassotti broke Luis Enrique's nose with an elbow to his face. The referee missed the infraction, however, and Italy survived.

Next up in the semifinals was Bulgaria, a team the Italians never expected to face. On a magical run of their own, the Bulgarians had upset Germany 2-1 in the quarterfinals. The victory came courtesy of the brilliant Hristo Stoichkov, who would go on to share the tournament's scoring crown award with Russia's Salenko. On this day, however, Roberto Baggio proved to be the best player on the field. His two first-half goals were all the Italians needed in a 2-1 victory.

Anticipation was high for the final, even among American sports fans, who were quickly learning to appreciate the artistry and excitement of a hard-fought soccer match. Brazil versus Italy was a classic matchup between a high-powered offensive machine and a well-orchestrated, suffocating defense. The Brazilians, going for their fourth World Cup, appeared strong and confident. Their defense had been a major story, allowing just three scores in six games.

The Italians, also on a quest for their fourth cup, were installed as underdogs in this game. Baggio had injured his hamstring in the semifinal match with Bulgaria, and was taking the field at less than 100 percent. Defensive stalwarts Tassotti and Alessandro Costacurta were also out, both due to suspensions. When Coach Sacchi turned to veteran sweeper Franco Baresi, who was still recovering from knee surgery, performed a mere three weeks earlier, Italian fans wailed in protest.

Perhaps because of the final's locale, the build-up to the championship game had the distinct feel of a Super Bowl. Singer Whitney Houston performed on the Rose Bowl field, and thousands of balloons were released towards the heavens. Unfortunately, like many Super Bowls, this game bored the sellout crowd to tears. This was unfortunate, for FIFA had been greatly encouraged by the reaction of mainstream American sports fans to this point. Although most did not fully understand the nuances of the games they were watching, ratings confirmed the fact that they were giving soccer on television a fair chance. A slam-bang final was all that was needed to hook millions of ticket-buying, jersey-wearing, beer-drinking, car-purchasing, Americans on soccer—and make pro soccer a commercially viable sport in the U.S.

Brazil and Italy had met four times before in the World Cup, and each game had provided plenty of memorable moments. This one definitely did not. Italy, playing without its best lineup, stayed back and waited for Brazil to make a mistake. Brazil,

Italy's Paolo Maldini attempts a tackle on Brazilian star Romario. The 1994 final was a tense defensive struggle from start to finish.

not wanting to press the action for this reason, probed the Italian defense for soft spots but lacked its usual aggressiveness. When Brazilian forward Jorginho went down with an injury 20 minutes into the contest, the team became even more conservative. The first half ended in a scoreless tie, as neither team managed to even take a good shot.

It was more of the same after the intermission. Neither Romario nor Bebeto could find space to maneuver for Brazil, while Baggio was blanketed by defenders throughout the second half and into overtime. With time running out the Italian star briefly brought the crowd to its feet when he found

himself with a clear shot, but could not summon the strength required to drive it past Taffarel. Thus for the first time ever, the World Cup final would be decided on penalty kicks.

Italy's Baresi stepped up first, and launched his shot over the net. Pagliuca covered for his teammate by saving a shot from Marcio Santos. Both teams scored on their next two kicks. Then Taffarel stopped Massaro. When Dunga found the back of the net, moments later, the Brazilians seized the advantage, 3-2. For Italy's last chance, Sacchi chose Baggio. Though obviously tired, he had carried Italy to the final with his magnificent play, and his coach looked

Romario exults in victory after Brazil's win over Italy in 1994. He was selected as the tournament's best player.

1998
France

In some ways it was odd that France was selected to host World Cup 98. Despite FIFA's best efforts, soccer never seemed to capture the imagination of the French people as it did the imaginations of the people in neighboring countries. That had something to do with France's years of frustration in World Cup play. During the tournament's long history, highlights had been few and far between for "Les Bleus." In fact, the French team had never advanced to the World Cup final. Although their passion for the sport itself remained undiminished, the French simply did not "get up" for the World Cup in the way they had before.

As host country, it would be a different story. The flame was reignited and every French fan was swept up in the excitement and spectacle of the event. Adding to this story line was the inexplicable controversy swirling around the national team. Like most squads, it featured several players who were either born in other countries or had roots in far-flung locales including Armenia, Ghana, and Guadeloupe. This was not unusual; international soccer rules have always been rather relaxed when it came to determining who qualified as a "native" player and who didn't. But with the world watching, some fans—and at least one prominent politician—complained that any victory would be hollow because France was essentially a team of foreigners.

to him one more time. With nothing left in his right leg, his shot sailed high and Brazil won its record fourth World Cup.

Although World Cup 94 had been decided by missed penalty kicks after a scoreless tie, on balance, the entire experience was a success. Contrary to predictions by the critics, the United States had been a nearly perfect host, and the tournament had been a major success. Scoring was up a half-goal per game, television ratings climbed way past projections, attendance soared to record numbers, and profits exceeded even the rosiest pre-tournament estimates.

The French soccer team, once criticized for having too many "foreigners," received few complaints after winning World Cup 98.

Most right-thinking citizens argued that France's multi-cultural club was one of the things that made the nation such a perfect choice to host the competition. The tournament had evolved to reflect the countries that competed in it, many of which were comprised of different ethnic groups. The varied makeup of the World Cup teams, most people felt, served to underscore how truly international the sport had become. Arguing over the "hollowness" of a French championship seemed stupid.

And pointless. After all, wasn't Brazil going to just roll over everyone? That was what the experts were saying. Brazil entered World Cup 98 as the overwhelming favorite. Champions four years earlier in the U.S., the Brazilians boasted the sport's deepest and most talented team. Their starting lineup read like an international all-star squad, with the world's top defender, Roberto Carlos, leading the way. If things were not going as planned, coach Mario Zagallo could turn to a bench that had reserves good enough to start for most of the other World Cup contenders.

Their ace in the hole was Ronaldo, the finest young striker in the game. Twice FIFA's World Player of the Year, Ronaldo was the youngest player ever to be named European Player of the Year. He was a breathtaking performer who could slice through opposing defenses with alarming ease. There seemed to be little question that Ronaldo would dominate the headlines for World Cup 98. Many fans felt he would shatter Just Fontaine's 30-year-old record for goals.

The only real threat to Brazil appeared to be the fact that more teams would have an opportunity to knock them off. The 1998 World Cup had expanded to 32 competitors, distributed into eight groups. Expected to be the toughest was Group D. Nicknamed the "Group of Death," it featured Spain, Nigeria, Bulgaria, and Paraguay—all very good national clubs. Argentina and Italy both seemed to have cake-walks out of their groups, while England, Germany, and Holland would likely encounter a bump or two along the way.

Among the more interesting early-round stories was the match between the U.S. and its bitter political rival, Iran. Team USA went down to defeat, which elicited little more than a national yawn in America, but set off wild celebrations in the streets of Teheran. A more compelling story was the first appearance in World Cup play of Jamaica. The "Reggae Boyz" captured the hearts of French fans with their enthusiasm and entertaining style of play. The hottest player in the opening games was Croatia's Davor Suker, who ended up leading the tournament in goals.

When French coach Aime Jacquet eyed his draw in Group C, he knew his team had caught a break. Denmark, South Africa, and Saudi Arabia had little or no experience in the World Cup. Though the French were still a longshot to win it all, the club boasted two of soccer's top stars in Zinedine Zidane and Lilian Thuram.

Zidane was rather amazing in his own quirky way. Off the field, few would have mistaken the ordinary looking and at times clumsy midfielder for an international superstar. Yet that is precisely what he was. The moment he pulled a jersey over his head he was transformed into Superman, with a fantastic ability to dribble in and out of trou-

ble, and create scoring opportunities where none seemed to exist. According to Zidane, Thuram was every bit his equal. A defender, he possessed a tremendous instinct for when to join the attack, but rarely found himself trapped out of position. With such a dynamic duo on his side, Jacquet felt anything was possible—especially if the home fans found a way to energize his team.

France certainly started on the right foot. Playing before a packed house in the Velodrome in Marseille, the team cruised past South Africa and Saudi Arabia. In both matches the defense—led by Laurent Blanc, Marcel Desailly, and Thuram—was

Zinedine Zidane veers toward the South African goal in first-round action from World Cup 98. The French star gained worldwide acclaim for his play in the tournament.

stupendous. Goal-keeper Fabien Barthez barely broke a sweat. The news wasn't all good, however. Zidane received a red card against Saudi Arabia for intentionally cleating the club's captain, Fuad Amin, and was suspended for two games. Meanwhile, striker Christophe Dugarry was carried off the field on a stretcher with a leg injury. France showed its mettle in the next match by beating Denmark 2-1 and moving on to the Round of 16.

Up next for the French was Paraguay which, along with Nigeria, had survived the "Group of Death." The South Americans weren't as fortunate against France. In a tense match, the teams entered overtime in a scoreless tie. With six minutes left in the ex-

tra period, David Trezeguet headed a perfect pass to Blanc, who fired a shot past superstar keeper Jose Luis Chilavert. This match was followed by another nail-biter against Italy in the semifinals. This time no one scored in regulation or overtime. The contest came down to penalty kicks, and France won, 4-3.

National hysteria was now spreading and intensifying with each heart-stopping victory. France faced off against Croatia in the semifinals. Suker opened the scoring for the visitors near the end of the first half. But Thuram, bolting up from his fullback position, answered less than a minute later. He added another goal in the second half to give France a 2-1 victory. No one was more surprised by Thuram's heroics than Thuram

Zinedine Zidane hurdles a Croation tackler in the semifinals of World Cup 98. France won 2-1 to advance to the final against Brazil.

himself. He had failed to score even once in 36 previous matches with the French national team! Four hundred thousand people lined Paris's Champs Elysees to cheer their heroes after the game. France was finally in the final. It was observed by many in the press that this outpouring of emotion was a sort of "victory parade," for five days later the team would be walking into the Brazilian buzzsaw, and almost certain defeat.

Yet Brazil's fans were nervous about the game, and understandably so. The road to the championship had featured an unsettling number of surprises. After demolishing Morocco in its first game, the team barely squeaked past Scotland and actually lost to Norway. Ronaldo seemed to sleepwalk through these matches, only to "wake up" against Chile with two goals a few days later. Brazil polished off Denmark and Holland in the quarters and semis, but not without some anxious moments. Indeed, there were times when these teams seemed every bit Brazil's equal.

France was absolutely electric for the final. The entire country shut down for the day, while some 80,000 fans poured into the Stade de France in Paris—among them President Jacques Chirac and Prime Minister Lionel Jospin. Long forgotten were the complaints about the "Frenchness" of the team; everyone was now focused on one thing: capturing the Cup.

As kickoff approached, there was indeed room for optimism. Brazil was a brilliant, dangerous team that was clearly out of sync. Which club would show up, the goal-scoring powerhouse or the tentative underachiever? France, meanwhile, was playing at a level it had never before come close to achieving. A team on a roll, playing before its home crowd, has a distinct advantage in international matches. However, France would be without one of its best players, Laurent Blanc, who had received a red card during an altercation with Croatia.

Soccer fans argued ceaselessly about the "key" to the game, but in the end most agreed that it would come down to Brazil's X factor: Ronaldo. On a good day he was capable of outscoring France singlehanded. But in the semifinal against the Dutch, he had turned his ankle and missed two practices afterward while receiving treatment. When Ronaldo woke up on the morning of the Sunday final, he still wasn't feeling right. Although the pain had largely subsided, he felt extremely sluggish and arrived at the stadium just a few minutes before his team was to take the field.

Ronaldo believed he was experiencing an allergic reaction to the medication he had been taking. There were also whispers that he had come down with a sudden case of nerves. The truth may never be known. However, by this time Zagallo had scratched his young star from the starting lineup, and only after much pleading and many assurances was Ronaldo reinstated.

In retrospect, it might have been better had Ronaldo just stayed in bed. His teammates were clearly unnerved by this strange episode. Sensing this, France went on the attack—normally a fatal error against Brazil. However, this time Brazil was caught by surprise, and they were unable to solve the French defense in the first half.

Much of the credit for this stinginess was shared by the inactive Blanc and his replacement, Franck Leboeuf. Blanc had been a teammate of Ronaldo's in the Spanish professional league and knew all of his tricks. He huddled with Leboeuf in the days prior to the final and schooled him on how

POWER PLAYER:
ZINEDINE ZIDANE—FRANCE

Zinedine Zidane can hardly believe it—"Les Bleus" are World Cup 98 champions!

Although the World Cup was started by a Frenchman, prior to 1998 you could count the country's World Cup heroes on three fingers There was Michel Platini, perhaps the best European player of his era, who fell agonizingly short of World Cup glory in 1982. And Raymond Kopa, the playmaking forward whose passes made a World Cup superstar of Just Fontaine (the third on this short list) in a losing cause during World Cup 58. Forty years later, Zinedine Zidane added his name to this roster.

Already considered the top French footballer, Zidane had distinguished himself as a hard-working, multi-talented field leader, first in France and then with the Juventus club in Italy. At World Cup '98, French fans pinned their hopes on these very qualities. Imagine their disappointment when, in Zidane's second match (a 4-0 shutout of Saudi Arabia) he received a red card for stepping on an opponent and was suspended for two games.

Zidane's teammates, forced to play without him, discovered they had learned a thing or two from their leader and made it to the quarterfinals on their own. Zidane rejoined the team in time to beat Italy and Croatia, which vaulted France into the final. There he enjoyed his finest hour, heading two corner kicks into the Brazilian net in a wild first half. Les Bleus went on to win the game and Zidane—the French-born son of Algerian parents—came to embody the racial unity that blossomed in France as a result of its amazing World Cup win.

to counteract the Brazilian's every move. Armed with this knowledge, the second-stringer played Ronaldo like he owned him, and totally took him out of the game.

Meanwhile, Zidane was all over the field. He was stronger and quicker than his opponents had anticipated, and unlike Ronaldo had risen to the occasion and elevated his game. In the 27th minute Zidane leaped high in the air on a corner kick from teammate Emmanuel Petit and headed a perfect shot past goal-keeper Claudio Taffarel. Eighteen minutes later, Zidane scored on a nearly identical play. This was a staggering development for Brazil, as the goal came during the extra time tacked on to the first half. It was one thing to go into the locker room down 1-0, but a 2-0 deficit was an entirely different matter. Ronaldo's teammates drifted under the stands, each deep in his own thoughts, each wondering what had gone so terribly wrong.

The scene on the French side was quite a bit different. Coach Jacquet assured his players that they would be facing a second-half onslaught by the world's most talented offense, and warned them about the dire consequences of taking this half-defeated enemy lightly. To start the final 45 minutes, Brazil came out attacking. But unaccustomed as they were to trailing so late in such an important match, the players pressed and performed with an uncharacteristic lack of discipline. At one point Ronaldo had a clear shot from in close at the French goal, and inexplicably booted the ball right at the keeper. That was Brazil's best and last serious scoring opportunity.

With 20 minutes left, Brazil's frustration began to show when their star Denilson was sent off the field. The team's last gasp came in the form of a great pass by Bebeto near the French goal, but Desailly calmly steered it aside before a Brazilian boot could touch it. Minutes later, in extra time, France's Petit put the icing on the cake with a final goal. The French won 3-0, dealing Brazil the worst defeat in its long and illustrious World Cup history.

Throughout France, the celebrations burned long into the night. Old-timers compared it to the end of World War II. At the Arc de Triomphe, as many as a million Parisian fans saluted their heroes. In this sea of humanity, little boys and old women wore the jerseys of their favorite players, without a thought as to "how French" they were. For a nation that had before courted only a passing interest in soccer, this was a spectacle for the ages.

> **Winner: France**
> **Runner-up: Brazil**
> **Best Player: Zinedine Zidane**

The French team makes its way down Paris's famous Champs Elysees during a wild victory parade.

2002
South Korea and Japan

World Cup 02 made history even before it began. The matches, held in South Korea and Japan, were the first ever hosted in Asia. As the tournament progressed, it became historic for the over-achieving exploits of perennial underdogs like Senegal, Turkey, South Korea, and the United States. When all was said and done, the two teams left standing were hardly tournament surprises. However, this was the only thing during the competition that did not shake up the soccer world.

The favorites going into the tournament included Brazil, Germany, Portugal, and Argentina, as well as the defending champions from France. The French team was hampered by a leg injury to Zinadine Zidane, and by its own complacency. The players seemed to be looking past their first-round opponents, and it cost them. Outhustled and outplayed by a plucky team from Senegal, France seemed a step behind all day in its opening match. A goal by Pape Bouba Diop gave the west African nation (once a French colony) an extremely satisfying victory, and sent Les Bleus into a tailspin. Zidane & Co. never made it out of their group, as Denmark and Senegal advanced.

Brazil also stumbled early on, with a loss to a good team from Turkey. But led by Ronaldo—now back in prime form—the team rebounded and won its group with key contributions from Roberto Carlos, Rivaldo, and Ronaldinho. The surprising Turks also advanced. Germany had an easier time of it. Relying on precision passing, tight defense, and the flawless goaltending of Oliver Kahn, the team won its group, too.

In the tournament's toughest grouping, Sweden and England slipped past Argentina. Among the other first-round survivors were Sweden (led by Henrik Larson), Japan (featuring bleached-blond star Junichi Inamoto), Spain (led by Fernando Morientes and Fernando Hierro), Ireland (behind Roy Keane), and England (which survived sub-par performances from Michael Owen and David Beckham).

The United States opened some eyes in the first round with an upset of Portugal. The Portuguese were led by Luis Figo, one of the best players in the world. But they were flat against Team USA, and paid the price. When Portugal lost to South Korea and its star Park Ji Sung, the boys from Lisbon were out of the tournament. The victory also enabled the Americans to advance. Two electrifying young scorers led the group winners: Landon Donovan and Ahn Jung Hwan.

The Round of 16 was one of the best in memory. With three of the five favorites already out of the picture, fans could not help but wonder if Germany and Brazil would be next. The Germans got a scare courtesy of the gritty Paraguayans but prevailed 1-0 on a goal by Oliver Neuville off a pretty cross from Bernd Schneider. Brazil, meanwhile, disposed of Belgium on goals from Rivaldo and Ronaldo.

The real fun came in the other matches. England's offense woke up against Denmark, with three first-half goals, including a spectacular score by Owen. Turkey continued to roll with a 1-0 shutout of Japan, and so did Senegal, which ambushed a solid Swedish team in overtime, 2-1. Spain nearly blew an easy win against Ireland, prevailing on penalty kicks, 3-2. South Korea won again, this time by a count of 2-1 against Italy. The victory threw the host nation into frenzied celebration. Down by a goal, the South Koreans pulled even on a shot by Seol Ki Hyeon just before regulation time ran out. In overtime, Ahn stole the spotlight with the game-winner. Meanwhile, America beat arch-rival Mexico, 2-0, to prove once again it could hold its own against the big boys of international soccer.

The quarterfinals offered a few surprises, but also reminded soccer fans who the true quality teams were. Turkey broke Senegal's spell with its persistent, measured attack. The Turks won in overtime when Umit Davala delivered a perfect pass to Ilhan Mansiz, who scored the only goal of the match. Despite defeat, Senegal's players left Asia beaming with pride. South Korea and Spain played to a cautious 0-0, tie which was won on penalty kicks by the South Koreans. Brazil erased an early deficit and beat England, 2-1. The Germans, though outplayed for much of their game against the U.S., escaped with a 1-0 victory.

With a Germany-Brazil final all but guaranteed, the four semifinalists took the field wondering whether World Cup 02 might offer the fans one more upset. Germany crushed the hopes of the South Koreans with suffocating defense, terrific goalkeeping, and a lovely header by Michael Ballack—the same player who beat Team USA—for a 1-0 win. In its game, Brazil had to contend with a very physical Turkish team. Surprisingly, the Brazilians pushed and leaned and tackled as hard as their opponents until Ronaldo scored the game's lone goal.

With Ronaldo playing brilliantly and Ballack forced to the bench by a second yellow card received in the victory over South Korea, Brazil was the favorite in the final. Germany's equalizer was Kahn, who thus far had been a stone wall in the net. Hoping to rattle their opponents, the Germans went on the attack early. The ploy produced the desired effect, as Brazil seemed totally discombobulated. Ronaldo stepped up at this point, breaking free for a dead-on shot against Kahn. Although his scoring attempt sailed wide, the Brazilian star's play emboldened his teammates, who now pressed the attack. Although the first half ended 0-0, the momentum had clearly shifted.

Kahn finally made a mistake in the second half, mishandling a long ball. Ronaldo was right there to boot it in, giving Brazil a 1-0 advantage. Twelve minutes later, Ronaldo was at it again. This time he found some space near the German goal and sent a shot screaming past a helpless Kahn. Brazil was crowned champion for the fifth time, and its young star was forgiven his sins of World Cup 98 and heralded as the planet's finest player once again.

Although the best players clearly won, it was unclear how much better they were than everyone else. There were far too many "upsets" in the tournament to be explained away by mere coincidence. Clearly, the gap was narrowing between soccer's traditional haves and have nots. Some experts claimed World Cup 02 marked the beginning of an important shift in the status quo. Others went farther, predicting that by World Cup 06 there would be a full-fledged changing of the guard. One thing is certain: There are more good players on more good teams than at any time in the tournament's long and glorious history. That's good news for soccer and great for the World Cup.

Champion: Brazil
Runner-up: Germany
Best Player: Ronaldo

WINNING WAYS

Heading into World Cup 02, some observers believed the Americans were a bit too cocky. The players themselves argued that this was nothing more than confidence—something Team USA had never taken into the tournament. But this was a different team. The squad had an experienced defense, plus plenty of youth and talent up front. Newcomers Landon Donovan, Clint Mathis, and Josh Wolff were a new breed of American player. From their earliest years in the sport, they had known almost nothing but success. Now graduated to the world stage, they expected to continue winning.

And win they did, against a pair of formidable opponents: Portugal and Mexico.

Portugal, the fifth-best team in the world, was Team USA's opponent in the opener. Led by reigning World Player of the Year Luis Figo, the Portuguese players expected a good match. What they got was a sound thrashing—despite the fact that U.S. captain Claudio Reyna was injured and unable to play.

Team USA caught a huge break early on when Portuguese goalkeeper Vitor Baia ran into a teammate off a corner kick by Earnie Stewart. The ball dropped loose in front of the goal, and John O'Brien blasted it home for a 1-0 lead. Twenty-five minutes later, the Americans got an even stranger goal—this one coming after Donovan drilled a crossing pass in front of Portugal's net. The usually reliable Jorge Costa tried to the head the ball out of danger. Instead he redirected it toward the near post. Baia then attempted to pop the ball over the goal with his fist, but it hit the crossbar and ricocheted in. Team USA later went ahead 3-0 on a lovely header by McBride. Though Portugal fought back, the Americans did a great job neutralizing Figo, and held on for a 3-2 victory.

Against host country South Korea, the Americans were hoping to win, but happy to survive. Late in the first half, Lee Eul Yong was fouled in the box, and only a brilliant save by Brad Friedel on the ensuing penalty kick kept the game scoreless. Mathis and O'Brien then teamed up to give the U.S. a 1-0 advantage. But Team USA surrendered its edge in the 78th minute after Ahn Jung Hwan outdueled Jeff Agoos, and notched the equalizer. The match ended in a 1-1 tie. After a dismaying loss to Poland, Team USA had to root for South Korea to defeat Portugal to avoid elimination. The tournament hosts obliged, scoring an upset that sent Portugal packing and America into the elimination round against Mexico.

The Mexicans had long dominated the United States in soccer, at one time boasting an unbeaten streak that stretched over four decades. But in recent years the Americans had taken five of six matches. Coach Bruce Arena fiddled with his lineup, knowing he needed fresh legs to contend with the dangerous duo of Jared Borgetti and Gerardo Torrado. The moves worked perfectly. The Americans counter-attacked brilliantly, and Reyna, back from his injury, played the best game of his life. McBride scored the first goal of the match off a gorgeous touch pass from Wolff. Donovan then put the game out of reach with 25 minutes remaining. The 2-0 final was America's biggest win in more than 50 years.

In the quarterfinals for the first time since 1930, Team USA squared off against Germany. Experts gave the Americans no real chance of winning. Man-for-man, the Germans were better at all 11 positions. They also had the intimidation factor on their side. At World Cup 98 they had brutalized the Americans. Reyna was kneed by Jens Jeremies with such force in that match that he was literally numb for 30 minutes.

Germany had respect for Team USA, but did not expect its opponent to press the action right away. Three times in the first half, Donovan eluded the defense and came close to scoring. But as good teams so often do, Germany recovered and struck back with a goal of its own. Down 1-0, Team USA attacked with renewed vigor in the second half. They came excruciatingly close to evening the score when Tony Sanneh headed a corner kick toward the left goal post. In the ensuing scramble, teammate Gregg Berhalter chipped the ball over goalie Oliver Kahn. Berhalter's shot hit the arm of Torsten Frings, who was standing near the post. Referee Hugh Dallas could have whistled a hand ball—which would have resulted in a penalty kick—but felt the touch was incidental. The German defense, startled and now deathly serious, squeezed the life out of the American attack and held on for a 1-0 victory.

Those who believe that success breeds success are looking forward to a good showing by the American team at World Cup 06. With maturity and experience, players such as Donovan and DaMarcus Beasley should be legitimate world-class players by then, while the rest of the squad will have four more years of international matches under its belt. Although soccer is becoming one of the nation's most popular youth sports, only now are the nation's best male athletes choosing it over the other team sports. With a solid development program in place, it might not be long before the U.S. is counted among the tournament favorites at World Cup time. When that day comes, fans will look back on Team USA's performance in World Cup 02 and realize that this was where it all began.

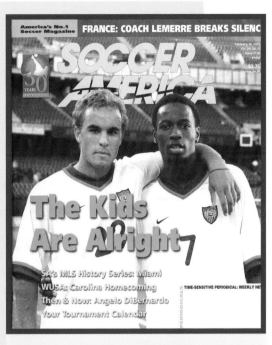

Soccer America cover boys Landon Donovan and DaMarcus Beasley should anchor Team USA for many years to come.

For More Information

Cantor, Andres with Arcucci, Daniel. *GOOOAL!*. New York: Simon & Schuster, 1996.

Pele with Fish, Robert L.. *Pele: My Life and the Beautiful Game.* New York: Doubleday & Co., 1977.

Galeano, Eduardo. *Football In Sun and Shado.* London, England: Fourth Estate, Ltd., 1997.

Gardner, Paul. *The Simplest Game.* New York: Macmillan, 1996.

Glanville, Brian. *The Story of the World Cup,* London, England: Faber and Faber, 1993.

Stewart, Mark. *Soccer: A History of the World's Most Popular Game.* Danbury, Connecticut: Franklin Watts, 1998.

Index

Page numbers in italics indicate illustrations.

About the Author

Mark Stewart ranks among the busiest sportswriters today. He has produced hundreds of profiles on athletes past and present and has authored more than 80 books, including all titles in **The Watts History of Sports.** A graduate of Duke University, Stewart is currently president of Team Stewart, Inc., a sports information and resource company in New Jersey.